Wealth Beyond Reason

Your Complete Handbook for Boundless Living

By

Bob Doyle

Boundless Living Publishing

Cover design by Dennis Kunkler
Cover photograph by Greg Mooney of
www.atlantaphotographers.com

A cataloguing record for this book that includes the U.S. Library of Congress Classification number, the Library of Congress Call number and the Dewey Decimal cataloguing code is available from the National Library of Canada. The complete cataloguing record can be obtained from the National Library's online database at: www.nlc-bnc.ca/amicus/index-e.html

TRAFFORD

This book was published on-demand in cooperation with Trafford Publishing. On-demand publishing is a unique process and service of making a book available for retail sale to the public taking advantage of on-demand manufacturing and Internet marketing. On-demand publishing includes promotions, retail sales, manufacturing, order fulfilment, accounting and collecting royalties on behalf of the author.

Suite 6E, 2333 Government St., Victoria, B.C. V8T 4P4, CANADA

Phone	250-383-6864	Toll-free	1-888-232-4444 (Canada & US)
Fax	250-383-6804	E-mail	sales@trafford.com
Web site	www.trafford.com	TRAFFORD PUBLISHING IS A DIVISION OF TRAFFORD HOLDINGS LTD.	
Trafford Catalogue #03-1738		www.trafford.com/robots/03-1738.html	

10   9   8   7   6   5   4   3   2

Praise for Wealth Beyond Reason

"Fantastic! The best book on manifesting wealth I've seen in decades! Read it and grow rich—beyond reason!"

Dr. Joe Vitale, #1 Best-Selling Author, "Spiritual Marketing"
http://www.MrFire.com

"For all those who seek the knowledge and techniques to create what you truly desire in life, this book is a must read. Bob effectively takes you through the process of creation, empowering you to take charge of your life. "

Ann Taylor – Inner Healing
http://www.innerhealing.com

"I **love** this book and can't recommend it strongly enough! The concepts in it are **so** incredibly powerful. This is THE book for anyone who desires to break free of struggle and live a life of abundance!! Life can be this easy! *Wealth Beyond Reason* shows you exactly how."

Suzie Dawson, Intuitive Coach
http://www.suziedawson.com

"Unwrap, open, and be open to the gift that Bob presents in *Wealth Beyond Reason*. It is your guide to 'having' it all and not wanting for anything. Be wizard wise and refer to this gift often, and you will plant the seeds that bring rich harvest ... from the fertile ground you have tended."

Marelin The Magician – Author of "Merlin's Message"

http://www.wealthbeyondreason.com/merlin.php

Dedication

This book is dedicated to You.

May you prosperously and abundantly share yourself with the World.

Acknowledgements

There are so many who in some way contributed to this book. I wish that I could tell you why each one was so significant, but that would be another book. So, with no intention to do any of them injustice, I will simply list their names here in no particular order, infused with the utmost gratitude for the role they have played in shaping my Life.

Some of these people helped inspire the content of this book. Others were there to put me on path and to keep me there, the value of which is immeasurable.

My wife Krissy, David Cameron, Toby Alexander, Tom and Penelope Pauley, Marelin Thornton, Kevin Underwood, Joe Vitale, Roger Lanphear, Suzie Dawson, Jason Mangrum, Amy Caffrey, everyone who came through my life at the *WishLift* event in Raleigh North Carolina June 9, 2001 (and you know who you are), my children Catharine, Deborah and Max, Claude Rifat, Jim Jones (not the reverend), Julie and Rick McKown, Marie Hallock-Sweet, Deb Britt, Lenny Rose, Ann Taylor, The Transforming Lifestyles Educational Center, and Chris Stratton, who first told me the Internet existed.

Table of Contents

Introduction to the Law of Attraction

Do you normally "skip" book introductions?

Please do not do that this time. This introduction sets you up for the whole book.

This book exists for one purpose: To explain to you as effectively as possible, exactly what you can do to **have everything in your life that you can possibly imagine**. And since that is such a tall order, I need to be able to explain how to do that in a way that does not seem "hocus-pocus" or require you to adopt some kind of "new-age" belief system, because I would lose a great many of those I am trying to reach if I went that route.

These principles are something of a "hidden secret" because although the world's wealthiest individuals have gained their wealth through the utilization of these principles, they have not always been consciously aware that they were doing so. In this book we reveal what all wealthy people have in common, and how you can easily model their process for attracting wealth of any level.

The trick here is that to explain how you can literally manifest (an interesting word that scares off more than its fair share of people) anything you can imagine – and furthermore to prove that it is, in fact your *duty* to do so - I need to get into some very unusual areas of science that are quite foreign to many people.

However, you are going to receive one heck of an education, and unlock your potential in a way that no other "self-help" book has ever been able to do for you in the past. You are going to finally learn why other approaches you may have tried in the past have failed to bring you the results you want. And actually, the reason is so simple! However, it is not so "easy" to explain.

I suppose I could be called a "prosperity coach", although I do not really feel comfortable with that term. One of the main reasons being that I have known a lot of "prosperity coaches" who are still struggling to make ends meets. They "know" the principles we will be discussing in this book, but have yet to fully integrate them into their own lives.

When I first discovered these principles in the way that I am going to present them to you here, I was really struggling financially. And I, like those prosperity coaches I mentioned before, was out there "talking the talk" about how you can create your reality, but this issue of *money* was still way out of my control. I believed (and still do) in what I was teaching at the time in terms of how to go about living your life by design, but there were some serious missing pieces to the puzzle.

I finally found those pieces, and I turned everything around in only a couple of months. I am going to show you how you can do the same.

I will share with you that being a "teacher" of these principles can be tricky business.

On one hand, I have the privilege of sharing what I believe to be the most exciting principles available for our use as human beings, because they truly give us access to *anything* we want. We are all "wizards in waiting", and we only need be awakened to our ability before we can literally wave our magic wands and experience anything we desire.

The other side of the coin however, is that the information I am going to share with you can be quite confronting. Because when it comes down to it, **your current situation – whatever that may be – is a direct result of what *you* are feeling, thinking, and believing.** Unless you can take full responsibility for where you are now, you will never fully have control over where you are going.

Many people do not like to hear that. They feel much more comfortable pointing at external factors and placing the blame for their situation outside of themselves. It is just easier that way. And society has given these people plenty of ammunition to support whatever beliefs of being limited they may have.

But if we were really "controlled" by external situations, it would mean that we really have no freedom to decide our own destiny. It would mean that our environment was the ultimate deciding factor as to whether we would succeed or fail. We would simply be "reacting" our way through life. But do you honestly believe that we were put here on this planet to simply react to our environment? Oh sure, some people "react" just fine and are quite successful without any knowledge of the Law of Attraction whatsoever. Nonetheless, **it is the Law of Attraction, which I will describe shortly, that determines their success**.

Many people, however, do *not* do well by living in "reaction". They consider themselves victims. They believe they were dealt a "bad hand". Or worse, **they simply do not believe they deserve the absolute best** that life has to offer. As a result, they run around in circles in victim mode, perhaps buying *libraries* of self-help books, saying to themselves, "I hope THIS works" not realizing that they have all sorts of self-defeating conversations running at a subconscious level that will render even the most effective self-help material totally ineffective.

This book will begin to change all of that for you.

You are deserving of whatever you want. You truly are. An entire chapter is dedicated to just this principle, and I believe it to be one of the most important truths you can come to understand.

This book is called "Wealth Beyond Reason" because it is truly *unreasonable* just how much wealth you can create using the Law of Attraction. At first, it may seem that what we talk about "defies logic", but in fact, it demonstrates perfect, scientific fact.

If you have ever seen someone with seemingly unlimited monetary resources and ever thought "they have so much money it is ridiculous", *that* is precisely the kind of wealth we are talking about helping you develop starting immediately. And **it is so simple, if you *let* it be.**

I also call this "Wealth Beyond Reason" because it is going to be your ability to "suspend reason" that allows you to have success with these principles. Many of us come from very analytic backgrounds and we have a hard time just blindly accepting new concepts, particularly if they seem to fly in the face of everything we have ever learned. Many of you will be confronted with these kinds of thoughts – and that is okay. It is people like you for whom this book was specifically written. And it is all built around this one crucial principle:

The Universal Law of Attraction

Energy Attracts Like Energy

As you begin to understand that *everything* in creation is based on a system of Energy - and when you learn some very basic things about how this Energy behaves - you will begin to unleash a creative force in your life that will seem miraculous. We will cover all this in detail!

This book is actually derived from an educational curriculum, also called "Wealth Beyond Reason", that we offer on the Internet. This Internet program allows a large group of "wealth creators" to share information with one another that helps us all to integrate these principles more fully into our lives – because we all see the tremendous value in doing so. And so shall you, as you read this book!

While much of the material in this book is drawn from the online material, I have the opportunity here to expand on the concepts even further. Still, I invite you to check out the "Wealth Beyond Reason" educational program at

http://www.WealthBeyondReason.com.

The reason I tell you about the online program, is because my life completely changed as a result of reading one of the books offered with that program.

The book is called "**A Happy Pocket Full of Money**" by David Cameron, and it is now the primary textbook in the "Wealth Beyond Reason" program. The shifts that took place in my life after reading that book led to the creation of the "Wealth Beyond Reason" online program. This, in turn, led me and others involved with the program down an incredible path of growth and discovery which has culminated in this first book.

The book you hold in your hands now can be thought of as a "milestone" in my own personal journey. It is an opportunity to share all that I have learned and experienced through using these powerful principles, and how your life can begin to change in a similar way.

Since adopting what you are about to learn into my own life, I have begun to attract outrageous things that are "beyond reason". **And only *sometimes* was money required**. The things that appear in my life without needing any money at all, continue to amaze me...because any "reasonable" thinker would logically assume that money – and a lot of it – was necessary to obtain such things.

This is why it is important to understand what wealth really is, and why the first chapter of this book answers that question.

Finally, please know that although the truths in this book are extremely exciting, this is not simply meant to be a "feel good" collection of material. My intention is to make a difference for you. But you have to take committed action to changing your current circumstances...and I will show you how.

Warning! Please read carefully!

The information in this book, when acted upon, truly unleashes powerful forces into your life, the effect of which is not always predictable, **but always for the higher good!**

Understand that by purposefully integrating these principles into your life, **you are inviting major change**.

If you have purchased this book because you are *ready* to make significant changes in your life, this book will help you do that in a powerful way.

But be warned...

Change **Will** Occur. Depending on your *final goal* this change may appear as though your life is falling apart around you – and in a way, that is an accurate assessment. But what you must understand is that if you follow the principles as outlined in this book, the Life awaiting you on the other side of this " clearing away" – and that is what it is – will be more joyous, prosperous, and perfect than you can possibly imagine at this moment.

Embrace the change, no matter the form. The Universe is doing your bidding in the most efficient way possible!

Part I

The Law of Attraction

It is my sincere belief that an understanding of how the Law of Attraction works in your life is some of the most important knowledge you can attain. When you understand the Law of Attraction, you gain incredible insight into your own Life, and why it is the way it is – and further, how to change it however you would like.

Remember that the Law of Attraction makes it possible for anyone to live their lives by total design. Making more money is just one small piece of the potential here, and is a lot less important than you think. Really.

Let us begin by getting a thorough understanding of what wealth really is...

What is Wealth?

And why do we *really* want it?

One of the reasons many of us have problems related to wealth is that we are all hung up about the **money**. We have erroneously equated having wealth with having money. One of the most important distinctions that you can make is that **money is merely a "symbol" of value**. But there are many other types of "value" available to you other than money that can be exchanged for what you want in your life. Further, as you will learn, the *last* thing you need to worry about is *how* you are going to get money to create the life you want.

Your only job is to know what kind of life you want to live the most, and to **find those things in your life that bring you the most joy, and keep your attention on those things**. That is really all you have to do. This whole book can be summed up in that one statement. Know what you want, and ask for it, then receive it. It is really so simple...and we as human beings are excellent at complicating it.

You are going to learn to "untangle" some limiting thought processes by discovering your true power...and it is awesome, by the way. You will learn a whole new meaning of the word "possibility".

At some point you will have this awesome "click"...or maybe a series of "clicks"...when you really, really *get* this stuff. When you suddenly realize that **anything you desire in your**

life can be yours - anything at all - Life becomes an entirely new experience. Then, you will really know what wealth is.

What you will learn is that "wealth" can be thought of in a couple of ways.

Monetary wealth will be a "by-product" of living the Life of your dreams…not the cause of it.

Read that again, because most people believe completely the opposite. Most people chase wealth so that they can "afford" the life of their dreams. What they do not see – and what you will learn – is that through living the life of your dreams, **you will literally attract exactly the resources you need to LIVE that dream**. That could mean a lot of money, or it could mean that some *other* means of delivery facilitates your "perfect life". It is your *openness* to various forms of delivery other than money that accelerates the process. It is a "letting go" of *how* things will happen, and I devote several sections of this book to Letting Go, because it really is such a crucial piece of all this.

Why do we really want "wealth"?

When it comes down to it, we are looking for a way to facilitate our *doing* what we most want to do. If we want to live in a big house on the lake, or own a luxury car, or even just a big screen TV, we have this idea that to get all those things we have to first get money. So we are looking for money to bring us those things, which has us looking in *totally* the wrong direction (regardless of your current logic), and we are slowing down the process of "having" immensely.

You *must* understand that *wealth* is not *money.*

Wealth is living the life you desire in abundance and joy (and that can include having a LOT of money)!

But wealth is not *about* holding on to a lot of money. Because remember (according to your current belief system) that if you do not *give* that money to someone in a business transaction, you will not get the thing you want. You are wanting money, *and* wanting to give away money at the same time!

"But I am only giving away the money to get what I want!" you say. Then why not stop spending all your Energy on "getting money", and instead put it on "what you want". You will save a lot of time that way, I promise.

I know it can be hard.

So if you *currently* equate money with wealth, I hope you will soon find your ideas begin to shift around as to what wealth *really* means to you.

In fact I will just warn you now: **You will probably experience a LOT of shifts...and some of them can be very powerful and/or confronting.** Simply decide to embrace these shifts as part of the growing process.

If something absolutely does not resonate with you, then you have no obligation to integrate it into your system of beliefs. I am not trying to change your belief systems or compromise values of any kind. This material should not challenge any kind of religious faith at all. In fact, I have heard from many people that these principles have *strengthened* their faith. This should be an exciting and joyous experience for you, albeit sometimes challenging!

You are about to learn how to **create whatever level of wealth you can imagine** - how to "create your reality" on every level - regardless of your past experience with wealth or alleged "evidence" that there is something wrong with your life as it relates to money.

You are about to be set truly free, but I first I want to ask a question to those of you who are having a hard time accepting all the things I am telling you...

Why Are We Skeptical?

And what is the cost?

I was a skeptic for most of my life. A real "show me the money" type of person. At the same time, there was so much I had always wanted to believe! There were many metaphysical topics that had always interested me, but I could never really "experience" any of them because of a basic skepticism that prevented these things from occurring in my life.

And of course, it had therefore always been my experience that **my skepticism turned out to be justified**. My belief system simply would not allow for extraordinary events, as if those were "too big" for me to tap into. It all just seemed too good to be true.

There are so many people who are ruled by the *too good to be true* mindset. And it is all about "being right". It is so easy to say that certain philosophies are not true, or that they are fantasy, because it is so very easy *not* to experience the truth of the extraordinary! You simply say it does not exist, feel it in your bones, and it will not! Therefore you have all the proof you need! And, it hardly matters what kind of evidence to the contrary might be presented to you. In *your* reality – the reality that you have attracted by your beliefs, thoughts, and feelings - you can support just about any belief (or disbelief) you have!

But does your skepticism truly serve you?

Personally my skepticism was a protection mechanism. After all, if I did not believe *anything*, I could not be disappointed! I could always be right!

But at what cost?

What I finally learned after so many years of yearning to experience new things, was that my active "disbelief" was the only thing keeping me from experiencing them. I could use all the logic in the world to "prove my point". But was I happy? No. But I was "right"...or so I thought.

Meanwhile, people everywhere around me were having the experiences I was wishing that I could have! What was the difference? Simple! They simply were not *resisting* the experiences.

The only reason you do not have everything you want in your life right now is because you are resisting it to some degree.

So you are thinking, "How can that be?" After all, let us say you really want a new house. You want it badly! How can you be resisting it?

By *wanting* it so badly!

First, the word "want", and more importantly, the *feeling* associated with the word, suggests an experience of "lack". You *want* It, because you do not have It. But the reality is that you *do* have it. It is right in front of you. You just need to "tune into" it.

I know that probably sounds very bizarre right now. Perhaps a little outside your comfort zone of beliefs. I understand that, and in fact, it is precisely why this book was written. I want to demystify all this, so that even the most skeptical among you can finally get your intellectual arms around these concepts, and begin to incorporate them into your life for your own benefit.

Yes, you will probably have to open your mind just a little. Just do it.

It is completely worth it.

So let us start with the most basic concept you need to understand at a scientific level...

You are Energy.

You vibrate and magnetize.

This concept is the key to understanding how these principles work. You do not necessarily have to understand all the ins and outs of Energy and Quantum Physics, but a basic knowledge of how Energy works can definitely help, particularly if you are of a skeptical nature! Energy after all, is what we are all made up of!

And please keep in mind: This is not a "physics" book, per se. The intricacies of quantum physics are completely and utterly mind-boggling to even very intelligent people. We do not need to understand the intricacies. We only need to know that it works.

Most of us do not contemplate how transistors and other electronic components "work". It is enough for us to know that they *do* work, in order to utilize them.

The Law of Attraction is the same way. It works regardless of your understanding of it.

You can look at anything in your Universe and break it down to its essence, which is Energy.

Your body. Your bed. Your dog. All are just various "configurations" of Energy.

You also need to know that **Energy vibrates at various frequencies**. In our human form, we experience things as "physical" if they fall into a specific range of frequencies. At higher frequencies, things become less "visible" to us. Thoughts, for example, vibrate at a very high frequency as compared to a chair, and are not visible to the eye. They exist, nonetheless.

To use another example, there are colors in the spectrum of possible colors that our eyes cannot see, but that *can* be seen by a snake. Dogs can hear frequencies of sound (also Energy) that we cannot hear. Those frequencies simply vibrate at a frequency that is out of our range.

Now I will stop right here for a moment to address what might occur as "awkwardness" around the word "vibrate". You might immediately think of some kind of hippie-speak ("getting bad vibes", etc.) and begin to discount what is actually one of the most scientifically exciting aspects of this whole exploration.

Energy vibrates at certain frequencies which "seek out" similar frequencies. Think of a guitar string. You pluck it, it vibrates, and it creates a certain tone. If there is another string in it is vicinity that is able to match that vibrational frequency, it will actually start to vibrate on its own. Tuning forks work the same way. It is all Energy; the string, the tuning fork, the sound, and the thought you are thinking right now about this whole concept. All Energy.

You are Energy, and you vibrate and attract according to your frequency.

Another thing to understand from all this is that nothing we see is actually "reality" (including money), but are our own **perceptions and interpretations** of the ocean of Energy all around us called the Universe. We are literally like radio tuners, and we "pick up" frequencies that vibrate within the range to which we are tuned!

Your energetic vibrations act like magnets to similar energetic vibrations.

If this is so, then what controls our vibrations? How do we "tune the dial" so to speak to match what we want?

It is your thoughts and emotions that dictate what you are vibrating, and thus, what you are magnetizing.

Here's an example you can probably relate to:

Have you ever had days that **started bad, and got worse?** It is very simply explained by the Law of Attraction. Something happens which you choose to interpret as "bad", which causes you to take on a negative emotion. This activates a magnet that will attract more of what will induce that emotion. So you burn your breakfast, hit every red light, get cut off in traffic, fight with your spouse...it just goes on and on. And it is no way a coincidence. It is what you have attracted.

The reality is you had a choice when that first "bad" thing went wrong to either have a totally different interpretation of the event, *or* to find something else on which to put your attention...something that brings you Joy! Once you do that, **the**

Law of Attraction will instantly begin to magnetize things that will perpetuate and build on that *positive* emotion. Good things will start to happen. And to the extent that you can amplify the joy you are feeling, things will only get better and better, rather than worse and worse. It is Law.

You see, the Law of Attraction does not "care"!

There is no "good and bad" to The Law. Those are strictly our personal judgments, based on our core beliefs.

The Law of Attraction simply responds perfectly to what you vibrate. The trouble is that as a society, we have learned to vibrate negatively. Our idea of "reality" is that life is hard, and that you must *work* hard for the things that you want. We have been taught that sometimes having good relationships means compromising who we *really* are to "make it work."

And to the extent that we adopt and integrate those beliefs, they will be absolutely true for us. They become true because all of our "evidence" will support these beliefs. Why?

Because the Law of Attraction will bring you more and more situations that are in vibrational alignment with your thoughts, beliefs, and most of all, your feelings.

You can see evidence of the Law of Attraction at work in your life everywhere you look. In fact, *everything you see is there as a result of you, attracting it into your experience.* Energy attracting like Energy.

That does not mean you consciously asked for a negative situation to be there. And do not confuse "attracting" your reality with "creating" it. Many people who are introduced to these ideas will argue, "Well, what about all the murder or war out there that is in my experience? Are you saying I created that??"

No.

However, there is no denying that you have attracted those vibrations it into your experience. You have allowed them in. It is not necessarily that you walked around *wishing* for murder and war. However, you were also not attracting a "reality" that was free of murder and war.

"But war is reality, Bob" you insist.

To the extent that you acknowledge it, yes.

Now before you get really frustrated with me, I will invite you to keep reading. This will all clear up as we go along, and we have an entire chapter called "Attraction vs. Creation" that will be of interest to you.

So if you did not ask for a negative experience, *how* did you attract it? And *if* you do not like what you have attracted, how can you attract something else? The answer to those questions is the key to attaining everything you can possibly desire in your life, and we have already touched on it a little!

But the first order of business is deciding what it is that you really want. You might be surprised to learn that those things you have always *thought* you wanted your entire life, are not necessarily your most important desires at all.

So let us figure out...

What do you <u>really</u> want?

It is not money. It really is not.

This book is about designing your Life. You cannot do that if you do not know what you want to design. So a logical first step is to figure that out.

For some people, this is easy. They can immediately tell you hundreds of things they want in their lives, and this is great! But what if you are so accustomed to having things you do not want in your life, that it is all you know! You have never even *allowed* yourself to think of what you *do* want because you are so busy "not wanting" all the other things in your life. And this is exactly why you *do* have those things you do not want. They are getting all your "magnetic" attention!

Remember the Law of Attraction: Energy attracts Like Energy. It does not attract "good" Energy or "bad" Energy. It attracts LIKE Energy. So if all of your focus is on what you do not want, then *more* of that is what you literally vibrate! Those vibrations are real magnets to more vibrations just like it! It is no wonder that your life seems to be an unending cycle of negative events! Why would it be anything else? You are not really asking for anything else!

But you say, "Oh yes I am! I have been asking for something different for years! I have been asking for more money as long as I can remember, and I *still* do not have any!" That is such a common statement, and there is so much about it that needs to be picked apart so that you can see exactly how **making such a statement *repels* the very thing you want to attract**.

First, we need to clarify that when we talk about you "asking" for something, we are talking about asking in a very specific way.

The key to getting what you want, is knowing how to ask.

Remember that this is all about being the best "magnet" you can be. Your vibrational frequency determines what you will attract, and it is all tied into the emotion you are feeling.

Emotion is the key. It is a unique Energy, and it is one that you can actually feel on a physical level. In essence, you can actually feel the magnet working.

If, when you "ask" for something, your request is wrapped in worry, then you are going to attract circumstances that perpetuate or even *grow* that feeling of worry.

For example, if you are asking for money from a place of "*Oh, PLEASE!* I **need** more money. I **do not have** enough to pay my bills! If I do not get more money **my life will be ruined!**", then think of what you are vibrating emotionally!

And believe me; I know it is not easy to simply *eliminate* the worry about money when all external evidence suggests that in "reality", there is a problem that needs to be solved.

I did not say it was going to be easy. I did say, however, that is it is simple. And it is. You "simply" have to ask for what you want in a way that you can feel positive emotion around it, rather than negative.

And it is not money you want.

"Oh, yes it is!" I hear you saying. Everyone says that at first, and generally for a long time. It is not that I do not understand that you honestly believe you need money. But I also know that money is not the thing you want to chase.

Your real desire is on the other side of the money. Remember that money, in and of itself, has no value unless we are all in agreement that it does. It is just paper and metal that symbolizes value that can be exchanged. If you are not using it to exchange value for something, it simply does not **have** any value! It is just the "potential" for exchange. **So your true desire is what you are going to acquire in exchange for that money!**

That could be paid bills, it could be a new home or car, or it could just be a nice meal out.

We have been taught that money is some kind of "ultimate prize". Yet, surely you have experienced times in your life when you received something that you wanted and it did not require money. You have been given gifts. You have won things, or you have seen others win things. You have in some other way come into a situation that has real value to you, but did not require that you exchange any money at all.

You would be amazed at how much of your life can be like that, if you will let go of feeling you need money to do everything.

"But I need money to pay the bills, Bob!!" I hear your brain screaming! And **I am not saying that you will not use money to pay the bills**. What I am telling you is that your focus – your *vibrations* – should be around the bills being paid…NOT around *getting* the money to pay the bills.

This frees the Universe up to deliver your desire (having the bills paid) in an infinite number of ways. Now, that way *could* be money! But if you decide ahead of time that "money" is the one and only way that you are going to have these bills paid, then you are also very likely to start looking at "logical" ways in your life through which this money will be delivered.

This even further **restricts the manner in which your ultimate desire could be fulfilled**. You will start to look at your job, a business, the lottery, etc. as potential avenues for this money to come. You are just complicating things by creating all kinds of unnecessary vibrations about the "rules of delivery", and it is not your concern at all!

In fact, if you "ask" for something, then immediately try to figure out how you are going to get it, you have effectively *revoked* the request. You are saying, "Never mind, Universe! I'll figure it all out for myself." And then you suffer over why it is being delivered so slowly or not at all! You are trying to intellectualize the process.

You and your Ego are not as smart as the Universe. So you will speed things up greatly if you will just step out of the way.

So how *do* you "ask" most effectively?

This is actually fully covered in the next section, which is "Design Your Life". And the really good news is that "asking" correctly is intrinsically easy and extremely fun. In fact if it is not, you are asking incorrectly!

The other good news is that there are many ways to ask correctly. And they all have one thing in common. They all bring the same net result, which is the raising of a positive vibration around your desires.

All the various methods have another thing in common. One of the first steps in all of them **is knowing what you want**. Understanding that it is not money is an important first step and will save you a great deal of time.

What will you do or buy with the money when you get it? How will you *feel* when you have those things? This is where to have your attention. It is a lot more fun to think about boating on the lake than thinking about how you are going to finance the boat, right? It is more enjoyable to think about cooking a great meal in your dream kitchen than trying to figure out what second job is going to pay for it. Get the picture? Good...because getting the "picture" is an integral part of the first step of the "creation" process.

Now it is time to find out what that process is...

PART II

How to Do It

You want to know the real kicker to all of this?

Your desires are already fulfilled. You are just not experiencing them.

"Huh?"

While it is a little complex to comprehend, you must understand that we live in a truly infinite Universe. We are experiencing only ONE of the infinite "realities" out there.

The reason we are experiencing the one that we are, is that this is the one with which we are currently in vibrational alignment. But ALL realities that you can imagine exist right now. You literally create their probability with your thoughts. To experience them, you need to simply "change your frequency", and this section is about how to do that.

By the way, we touch more on the idea that your desires are already fulfilled in the section called "Your Desires are Already Fulfilled" found in Part III, Technical Support.

Designing Your Life

How to ask for exactly what you want... and nothing less!

This is the fun part! At least it is supposed to be! In fact, if it is not fun, it probably will not work. Taking this process too seriously will backfire almost every time, and I will get into why as we go through the process.

There are basically a handful of steps to the process. This process is repeated in various ways by different "Law of Attraction" authors, but the essence is always the same.

The process can be broken down into just a few steps, which follow. They are the same steps everyone else gives you, and I have added the benefit of my experience in their description.

And by the way, as you are starting out in all this, you have to know that you cannot "skip steps". You have to do them all.

With practice, the steps will flow much more naturally from one to the other, and it will not have to seem like such a "process". But you are learning something new, and un-learning *years* of false information. Take as long as you need. You Deserve It!

Step 1 – Be Clear on What you Do NOT Want

Knowing your true desires in life can be really easy, or it can be a huge challenge.

It is amazing to me how many people struggle with knowing what they want in their lives. We are actually taught that there are "reasonable" goals, which usually fall short of what we consider our "wildest fantasies".

But we have those fantasies for a reason: **They are ours to experience.**

For some of us, it is hard to decide what we *do* want because we have just never been trained to dwell on it for very long. However, it is usually *very* easy to identify what you do *not* want, and that is a great place to start!

Many people dwell in what they do not want. They wallow in it! In fact, it consumes them!

"I do not want this debt!"

"I do not want this relationship!"

"I do not want this extra weight!"

Well, I hate to break it to you, but the Law of Attraction *demands* that if you put all your focus – or more accurately – all your *emotions* around these thoughts, then you are certain to get more of the same!

However, knowing what you do NOT want can easily lead you into:

Step 2 - Know What You DO Want and Write It Down!

Knowing what you do not want is the best way to know what you do want. So when you have those "do not want" feelings, immediately ask yourself what the **opposite** of that would be. You do not want your broken down car? Then immediately imagine the car that will bring you the most joy!

It is very important to begin to bring your thoughts of what you want into the physical in some form, and there are several ways to do this. Many people find pictures that represent what they wish to attract, and make a collage. Others put those pictures in box of some kind. Still others make a detailed list, which I highly recommend.

All of these methods work wonderfully. You are creating a "point of attraction", and the process should be exciting, even exhilarating to go through! As you begin to "flesh out" the parameters of what you truly desire, your vibration will shoot sky high and you will be magnetizing like crazy! You will be absolutely amazed at how quickly things will begin to show up.

The caveat, of course, is that you completely release any responsibility for figuring out how these things will come. You must let go completely of trying to control the situation.

This is definitely the tough part. We want to be in control. It is hard for us to imagine that by doing nothing, we gain everything. This is actually "Step 4" of the process. But before we get there we have to know precisely what we are letting go of! And that means **making your list** (not in your head, but on paper) of what you want.

I have coached hundreds of people through this process. I cannot tell you how many e-mails or phone calls I get that go like this:

"Bob, I have read all the books, and listened to all your seminars and things just aren't improving! It just is not working!"

"Have you made your list?" I reply. "Have you actually written down exactly what you want and the feelings associated with having it?"

I can tell you that the answer is "No" nearly 100% of the time.

Now, how hard is it to take out a pencil and paper and write down a list of things you truly desire? Well, apparently it is pretty hard for some people, because they just do not do it. It is the classic "self-improvement" approach: *Read a book, expect miracles.*

It usually does not work that way. BUT, the way it *does* work is not hard! This process is really a great deal of fun, once you actually start! It is like anything else, though. Starting seems to be the hardest part. Perhaps you want so much that the thought of writing it all down is overwhelming! So you keep it in your head, thinking that is good enough. For most it is *not*, for several reasons:

1. Writing things down brings your desire into physical form.
2. Writing helps you gain clarity, and further refine your desire into something you absolutely know you want.
3. Writing allows your desire to "stand alone", without being surrounded by the clutter that normally exists in our thoughts regarding what we want.

Until you actually do this, you will never know how powerful it is. Unfortunately, most people see this as *much* too easy, and do not believe that something so simple can bring them what they want.

And they'll never know, will they? Unless they actually do it.

Step 3 – Experience Your Desire Fulfilled

So what does this mean?

To "experience" your desire fulfilled means to put your current thoughts and feelings in a state that would suggest that you have already achieved your dream! If you can generate the same emotions that you will have when your desire is fulfilled, you align vibrationally with the reality of the desire fulfilled, and thus become a magnet to it.

Please re-read that. It basically means that by simply experiencing the emotion of having your desire fulfilled, you begin to draw the *reality* of those feelings to you through the Law of Attraction.

This requires some degree of visualization, though that does not necessarily mean you have to "see images" in your imagination, though that helps immensely. What you want as an end result is that through visualizing what it is like to have your desire fulfilled, your mind and body actually respond physically in an emotional way. That is, you change your vibration. You can actually feel it if you even slightly tune into it.

As you visualize, or imagine, you want to conjure up a reaction from every one of your five senses, as well as those senses, like emotion, that are less tangible.

You want to SEE, HEAR, FEEL, SMELL, and TASTE your desire being fulfilled.

And the key is to *stay in that state as long as possible.*

But how do you get in that state in the first place?

If you normally find yourself in an environment that really provides little positive reinforcement, it can be quite challenging to generate the kind of imagery I am talking about.

Writing things down really helps, however.

You might also consider a practice such as meditation. Meditation, while used for many purposes and having many disciplines, is an excellent way for you to accelerate the manifestation process.

Meditation allows you to quiet the mind so that it is easier for you to direct your attention as you wish, rather than being bombarded by a lot of noise and screaming from the Ego that "you can't possibly have all these things you want!"

Mediation techniques abound. You can find them everywhere. Some are as simple as merely putting your attention on counting your breaths while in a comfortable position.

But for those with really noisy minds, and who are in a hurry, there are alternatives.

For example, part of the "Wealth Beyond Reason" online program is an audio meditation that uses "brainwave synchronization" technology to induce the meditative state in the listener with no effort on their part. And there are many other such offerings available in the marketplace.

There is "hardware", such as "light and sound goggles" that also helps to induce the meditative state.

Whichever approach works best for you, use it! While in the meditative state (depending on how deep you go), your **visualization ability is greatly enhanced**, and you will find that it is much easier to "be" that your desire has been fulfilled!

The more time you spend in this state, the more "magnetic" you are. See the section in "Part III" called *In the Face of All the Evidence* which touches on how even a few minutes a day can be of benefit to you, unless you immediately start "reversing" the work you have done after you end your visualization session.

You would reverse your results with statements like "Well, back to reality!", or "Well, that was nice, but now I'll go back to feeling worried about money."

Remember that you will attract in relation to your most predominant vibration! What you are thinking about the most will become your prevalent reality!

We are working to change the balance of the scale. So start as slowly as you would like, but *start.*

This is all about raising your vibration. It is about "feeling good".

As I stated earlier, it really comes down to knowing what you want, requesting it, and then finding something to feel good about, so that you are vibrating at a higher frequency for longer periods of time. See the section called *Raising Your Vibration* in "Part III" for more on how to do this.

Now that you have your desire clearly in mind, and you are giving yourself time on a daily basis to bask inside the wonderful feelings of the desire being fulfilled in this moment, it is time for:

Step 4 – Let Go and Allow

Without question, this is the hardest part for most people to get a handle on. After all, how can you *want* something with all your heart, and then totally detach from it? How can you suddenly *not care* if you get it or not? Tricky business to be sure, but it does not have to be as hard as it sounds.

First, letting go does not mean to stop wanting what you want. That would be pretty silly, wouldn't it? "Letting go" means a couple of things:

1. Have no attachment to the means by which your desire will be delivered. Leave it to the perfect scientific system to deliver! Do not try to figure it out. Do not work harder. Do not look for any specific thing to make it all possible – like an increase in business, or winning the lottery. You must allow ANY possibility, and realize that **your desire may very well be fulfilled in way that you could never imagine**...and that is precisely how it happens so much of the time. You might get an unexpected opportunity to make some extra money...someone suddenly may want to give away their car (and yes, that certainly happens), or you receive an unexpected gift. These are just a few examples. But you need to be open to anything.

2. You have to **not care** whether you get your desire or not. That does not mean to get into a state of resignation. You should still be excited! But also know that the Universe can deliver even BETTER than what you expect! So, you

just have to keep all your options open! Be ready for **anything!**

"Not caring" simply means that you do not put any "care" towards the desire, because there is no need. You already know it is going to be fulfilled. So what is there to "care" about?

Pages and pages have been written about this idea of detachment by Law of Attraction practitioners, because it is truly one of the hardest things to do. But you must, you must, you must.

If you are constantly "obsessing" over your desire, then what you are truly doing is constantly reminding yourself that it is not here! This will generate a very specific feeling, and it is *not* the feeling that will attract your desire. The more "life and death" you feel your desire to be, the more you repel it! Instead, joyously accept and allow the Universe to bring it to you at the perfect time, and in the perfect way.

When it comes down to it, detachment comes from a total "knowing" that what you want is coming. After all, when you order food in a fine restaurant, you do not fret as to whether the waiter is going to bring you what you want. There is no doubt in your mind. You are completely detached.

And so it can be with your desires once you fully trust in the power of the Law of Attraction. You ask for what you want, you know it will come, and you do not give it a second thought. This will speed the manifestation of your desires like nothing else, because you truly will not care a lick about the "when" and "how", and you will not be forcing the Universe into taking any particular path in delivering, which can really slow down the process.

And how do you "force" the Universe to deliver in a certain way? Well, remember that you attract that with which you are vibrationally aligned. If you are only vibrationally aligned with things coming to you in a certain way, then you are blocking out all other avenues through which your desires can be fulfilled. That translates into you missing out on all sorts of opportunities that might arise.

Instead, if you are vibrationally aligned with "any and all" possibilities – "This, or something better - for the good of all concerned", you have created a much larger valve through which delivery can be funneled!

The best way to start deliberately creating is to ease into it by manifesting something small. Choose something that you can get excited about, but that you truly do not care whether it comes to you or not. You have no "time deadline" in your mind. Choose something that does not seem so monumentally impossible that your mind will constantly be having a conversation about how unbelievable the idea is, which will make it virtually impossible for you to maintain the magnetism you want!

It is much easier to "let go" of the little things. As you have success, you will be able to translate that ability to the larger ones.

Once you have truly let go, you are in a perfect state of "allowing" the Universe to deliver through the most efficient means possible, since you are not going to be looking for it to come in any particular way...*are* you?

And That is It!

It really is that simple.

Simple...though not necessarily *easy*.

While these principles truly are quite basic, our lifetime of building self-defeating Energy systems throughout our minds and bodies often makes even these simple steps a daunting task.

You are very likely to run into all kinds of subconscious and even conscious "blocks".

The rest of this book is dedicated to getting past those sticking points. This really boils down to getting your attention completely off what you do not want in your life, and completely *on* what you do want. These "blocks" work against you, by shifting your attention where it does not serve you.

Eliminate the blocks, and you are free to create without restriction! I call the final section of this book "Technical Support". But before we go there, there is one more concept you need to fully incorporate into your life:

Give, And You Shall Receive

We have heard for years about how we "should give". We have learned that it is a nice thing to donate to charity, and to help those less fortunate than us in a number of ways.

Many people give freely and with a joyous heart. These people are richly rewarded, as I will share with you shortly.

Others share begrudgingly. A sense of obligation squeezes their giving out of them, and there is a sense of "loss" associated with the giving. "Well, there's money I'll never see again. I hope they make good use of it!"

Still others do not give at all, completely ruled by the belief that they absolutely cannot afford to part with even the slightest amount of money, for fear that they will "lose everything" if they do.

Which group do you think the Law of Attraction benefits the most? Pretty obvious, isn't it?

The last group is living in fear of lack. They are vibrating this "fear of lack" frequency constantly, and thus the Law of Attraction delivers exactly the circumstances that will substantiate that fear! It can do nothing else! It does not choose what comes to you. You do the choosing. The Universe, through this simple principle of physics, simply "reacts" perfectly to your "request".

Thus a person who does not *give* out of fear of "not having enough to spare" will perpetuate the reality that they do not.

I know of many people who fall into that last category, who decide to "try giving to see if it works", in terms of creating a positive flow of money into their lives.

This puts them into the second category of person I described above. Their actions indicate giving, but what they are vibrating is still worry, doubt, and fear. Even if the feeling is not very strong and obvious, the Energy system is running, and it is repelling the "return on the investment." And then, when no return seems to come, they get discouraged, and then find themselves back in the last category of people who do not give, because their "evidence" is that giving does not result in receiving.

However, those who give freely and cheerfully, generate their rewards in numerous ways.

Have you noticed that some of the richest people in history have also been those who gave huge sums of money (and time) away? The logical response is, "Well, sure! They can AFFORD to give. They're rich!"

The point is that it is the other way around.

Many people talk about the "cyclical flow of Energy" that comes from giving, but when you get down to it, it is really no more than the Law of Attraction at work. You can see for the people in the second and third group, "giving" does not necessarily result in receiving. The difference is in what the giver is "vibrating" about their giving. It is no more complicated than that.

In the case of the group one "free-givers", there is a lot of positive emotion around their giving. The Law of Attraction dictates that this emotion will attract more of the same, and at an exponential rate. So if you are vibrating true joy in giving, you will attract more experiences that allow you to experience that joy – but in an even bigger fashion!

To facilitate grander giving (to make it possible for you to give more), what would have to happen? You would have to *attract more to give!* Which means the Universe will facilitate that for you. You do not have to figure out HOW at all!

If I could instill ONE principle into your head forever, it would be the fact that **you do not have to figure out how anything will happen**. It will happen because you follow your intuition and passionate feelings. It will not feel like "work", and you will not have to suffer over it one bit.

Practically nothing else will bring you what you want, faster than giving what you want away.

Except perhaps for one thing:

Gratitude

Gratitude works in your favor much the way that Giving does. By generating strong feelings for the appreciation for what you have, and what you *will* have, you attract the circumstances that will facilitate more of those feelings.

So when you are truly grateful – meaning that you bathe in the feelings of being truly blessed with what you have – you will attract more things for which to be thankful. You have created a "space" for more things to come to you that will make you FEEL gratitude.

See, it is really simple! There are entire books on gratitude, and we just summed up why and how it works in a couple of paragraphs!

So since it is all so simple, you are just going to go out and manifest your dreams overnight, right?

Well, I hope you do! You now have everything you need to know summed up in less than 60 pages!

Now, on the off-chance (big wink) that you do not create the life of your dreams overnight, you can always refer to our "technical support" section, which follows.

Part III

Technical Support

Your Reference Manual
For Getting Through the "Sticking Points"

The following chapters are taken from a few of the audio seminars from the "Wealth Beyond Reason" Internet program. They will serve to help you through the "sticking points" you may encounter along the way.

It would be nice if simply having this intellectual understanding of the Law of Attraction would give us the ability to start manifesting everything we desire right away. And make no mistake: that is entirely possible. In fact, my ultimate goal is for each of you to become absolute Masters at this, decreasing the time from "expressing your desires" to having them realized, more and more each day.

*But we have got a lifetime of "stuff" going on that slows us down. Let us look at the most common "stops" people run up against - **starting with what you do for a living.***

The Most Important Value You Can Give

In this book, we talk about Giving and that *how* you give directly determines what you receive, many times over. And "giving" is just another way of saying "put out vibrations". We can put out these "giving" vibrations by direct exchange of value through money, or through our time, or – and this the real point with this chapter – *just by being who we truly are*, rather than playing our society-given *roles*.

If we want to receive anything in our lives – and that can be money, relationships, or just "stuff" – we have to provide value to the Universe, and we do that in the form of positive vibrations. So what we are vibrating throughout the course of the day is extremely important because it directly influences our moment to moment experience.

So, what are we doing "most of the day" that is going to dictate what we are vibrating out there? Because remember, it is one thing to do "wealth consciousness meditations" a couple of times a day for maybe an hour, but that is a small fraction of our waking day. If we are not very conscious about all this, especially at first, it is going to be our "non-meditating" thoughts, if you will, that dictate what comes into our lives.

So what does this mean? Well, for one thing, if you are working at a job that is unsatisfying, or you are otherwise unhappy with the occupation that takes up 8+ hours of your day, **that is a lot of time to be vibrating at a low or negative frequency**, isnt' it?

If your "wealth consciousness" coat gets checked at the door of your workplace, then you are really sending the Universe mixed signals about what you perceive the reality of your life to be.

You wake up in the morning and spend time envisioning your perfect life, you get into the feeling, and all that stuff that is helping to accelerate fulfillment of those desires. Then you think, "Ok, back to the real world. Gotta go to work", and for the next 10 hours your thoughts are mired in a wholly unsatisfying pattern of thought which of course, simply works to attract more of the same.

And how much of your true value are you really contributing, when so little of the "real you" is in your work? Not much! Therefore, you are not *due* much "return", despite the hours of labor you are putting in.

The hours are not the value. Value is not gauged by how hard you work. Value comes from answering this question: **What is your contribution to the Universe?** This is a more accurate assessment of value, because the quality of your "contribution", or your Energy, will improve as you live the life you truly desire to live, instead of the one you have been "railroaded into" inadvertently.

But you say, "I *have* to go to work, though! Until these principles start kicking in, I have to pay the bills somehow! I can't wait for the Universe to deliver. I need money now!"

This type of "flip-flop" thinking can be directly attributed to our friend the Ego. And it is just so easy to listen to its logic sometimes, is it not? I mean, there IS a bill sitting there, right? Somebody is demanding money from us, right?

It is the attitude, or more accurately the *emotion* associated with the defensive statement of "I have got to pay my bills!" that is getting you into trouble. Like, "I love this system when it works, but when it does not, I feel like an idiot for wasting my time." Well, I am happy to say the Law of Attraction does not pick and choose. The Universe delivers EXACTLY what you order, whether you do it consciously or not.

So what is the obvious fix to this "job" thing? Well, it is simple. Find out what you love to do, and do that. The obvious objection comes, **"I'd love to, but it will not pay the bills"**, which of course, makes that defensive excuse completely true for whoever says it.

"But BOB! I have *tried* living my dream! I have *tried* doing what I love to do, and I about went broke!"

I have been there.

But here is what was true for me, and I would ask you to look closely at this: When I first was out there trying to make a living at what I "loved to do", it immediately became a **job**. Something felt "at stake". There was a "do or die" about it. Some of the passion and joy of the activities (and I tried several) was sucked right out because I suddenly "needed to make money with it".

What is the effect on your vibration when you engage in this kind of thinking? It plummets. You are now vibrating with stress, fear, and worry.

And while in your previous attempts to live your dream, you may have had fun...but were you aware of the Law of Attraction? Did you have a clear vision of the life you truly wanted to design? Or were you going through your day-to-day, doing what you loved, with no clear direction, or with an idea in the back of your mind that this may not all "pan out" they way you want?

Really think about this, because the answer to why it did not work in the past lies in the honest answers to these questions. If you had no clear vision, then raising your vibrations by doing what you loved only served to bring you more of whatever it is you were vibrating, or thinking about. If you were not creating a future vision, then your thoughts were probably just on your day-to-day activities. So you remained wherever you were. And then, when you did not see "progress" – even though you really did not define (and FEEL with positive Energy) what progress was – then, your Ego started to second-guess your decision to "do what you loved" for a living.

The moment that happened, you began the descent. Because you were not consciously aware that you should have reversed that thinking immediately, you just followed this counter-productive thought process downward, which resulted in a manifestation of negative situations. Then you made the conclusion, "Well I tried it, and I failed." And you started looking for a new "real job"...when that was totally not necessary, and almost decidedly not the way to wealth, particularly if you simply settled for a job that did not fulfill you.

Here is the big secret: **Be who you are!** Do what you are *meant* to do without worry or apology. As a result, your vibration will naturally rise and your predominant thoughts, desires, and intentions will come to you more rapidly. Why? Because you will put out no higher vibrations – you will contribute no greater value to the Universe as a whole – than when you are being fully and completely who you truly are, contributing your natural unique gifts to the world, and loving virtually every moment of your life! The reward for that is your ability to live whatever life you want. Pretty nice reward, I'd say.

Does God Deserve What He Wants?

In my opinion, the fact that you actually "deserve" everything you could possibly imagine is one of the most important truths you can gain from reading this book.

If there is a "governor" that controls how quickly you will manifest your desires, it is the extent to which you believe that You Deserve What You Want.

I want to ask you a question, and I really want you to think about it: **Does *God* deserve what he wants?**

Well obviously, your answer is most likely "Yes" – unless the very concept of God is an issue for you. In that case, I would simply ask you to consider that *some* force designed this Universe and All That Is in It. Some intangible intelligence arranged these intricate systems of Energy in such a way that you and I, in this human form, are able to experience something that we call Reality. For the purposes of this conversation, we are calling that intelligence God.

Now, if this Intelligence arranged All That Is – if it was "their idea", so to speak – do you not think this intelligence deserves what it wants?

Now consider part of what I just said – These systems of Energy that compose *everything?* We are a part of that. **We are an extension of this intelligence.**

At a most basic level, we are a system of Energy that "manifests" itself into cells, tissue, organs, and so on, into the form of a human being. And with all these cells, tissues, and organs, **we are given the ability to experience a wide range of** *other* **Energy Frequencies around us.**

We experience these frequencies as things "outside" of us – like chairs, houses, money, other people, etc. but they are not *outside* us, as much as they are a *part* of us. We experience the illusion of separateness, because the frequency at which our Energy is vibrating, is literally magnetically attracting Energy vibrating at a similar frequency. We bring into our experience those things that we magnetize to us.

And how do we magnetize? By now, you know it is through the power of our thoughts and emotions that we actual generate magnetic Energy. We have been given this incredible gift of *imagination*, and tied closely to that is the gift of Emotions. Emotions allow us to experience our "reality" in ways that many other configurations of Energy, like a table, cannot.

We can feel joy, exuberance, and passion! And doing so will attract Energy to us that will cause us to feel more of those feelings. This Energy can be in the form of other people, things – like cars and homes – or any other experiences that you desire!

On the other hand, we can choose to feel fear, pain, sadness, guilt, or jealousy, and thus attract Energy that manifests as an environment that will sustain *these* feelings. But it all begins with our choice. But there are many facets to our choice!

On the surface, our choices seem so simple:

"I want a new car. I choose that Mercedes right there."

However, below that surface description of our want, there are many other conversations being had, such as:

"But I do not have enough money", or "I do not really *need* it, I guess", and the one that most people do not even know they have: "I do not Deserve that car."

All of these responses are false. They have been learned by you throughout your experience, simply because you did not know any better. Somewhere along the line, you were exposed to Energy systems – perhaps in the form of parents, friends, or your physical environment - which instilled these thoughts as beliefs. But remember, the truth is that you are a magnificent configuration of Energy that has the ability to manifest into its experience – *your* experience – whatever you desire. But your desire has to include your **allowance** of its fulfillment. Those thoughts like, "I can't afford it" and more importantly, "I do not deserve it", are exactly what is stopping you from that fulfillment.

No thoughts are as Universally prohibitive than "I do not deserve it." If you do not feel you deserve something, no other thought you will have will override that.

If you are truly vibrating that you do not deserve something, it cannot be attracted to you, at least not for any extended amount of time.

On the other hand, if you *do* feel that you deserve something, it is much easier for you to allow it to flow into your life.

There is an important distinction that needs to be made here. Truly feeling you deserve something by divine inheritance is much different than taking a position that you *think* you deserve something because you did this or that "nice thing", and that somebody somewhere ought to give you what's coming. This thought process is based on a lack mentality, or one of earth-level "fairness".

Deserving, as we are talking about it, has nothing to do with thinking you should have something "because you did this great thing and you should be compensated". For example, you do not deserve what you want because you are a good person, or because you give to charity, or because you have worked your fingers to the bone for decades and the time has come for the payoff.

You deserve what you want simply because it is the intention of the Creator that you *experience* your desires. Your passions exist to show you the way.

You are designed to have what you want, because it is through your experience of the joy that you derive from *having* those things that fulfill your desires, that the non-physical God (or whatever terminology with which you are most comfortable) **enjoys** the experience of the physical which He has created.

Your desires are a gift to you. They tell you your purpose. They tell you precisely what is intended in your life. It is only our limited thinking that prohibits us from experiencing those things immediately. We have learned that we must "work for them", or "earn them", when the truth is, "Ask, and you shall receive."

But we as humans have attached this false meaning to the word "deserve". We have decided that someone must validate us, or that we must validate ourselves based on things we do, how successful we are, how hard we work, or a countless number of other man-made metrics by which we gauge our worth.

It is very simple, really. It is just that it seems very complex to deal with, because we are such complex forms of Energy – we have allowed our memories, beliefs, thoughts, and emotions to define who we think we are. But we are truly more than all of those things. They simply determine our experience. And all of those are flexible. They are pliable and liquid. They are thoughts that you are having in this present moment. They may occur to you as the "past", or what you believe your future will be, but in actuality, they are simply how you are choosing to interpret the sum total of your experience of the Universe, in this moment. So it is *in this moment*, that you can change everything.

But you have to start with knowing that you deserve what you want. For when you do, there is absolutely nothing stopping you from having it.

On the surface, you might not even be aware that you have any issues with "deserving". But what I can assure you is that if there is something you want in your life that you do not yet have – and particularly if you have wanted it for a long time – and even *more* particularly if you have been working with the Law of Attraction to get it - it is most likely because at some level you feel you do not truly deserve it.

Think about it. If God, or this Omniscient force of which all things are made, has a true desire, do you think there is any delay in its fulfillment? Of course not. And, *we are extensions of this creative source.* We do not *have* to wait, except to the extent that we feel that we "should" and that is based on the extent to which we feel we *deserve* what we want. Perhaps we feel more deserving of things if we work a little longer...or if we are a little nicer to people. Then, we feel that we Deserve what we want, and only then do we allow it into our experience through a vibration that fully resonates with what we desire.

This is a hidden issue for many people. We get started with the Law of Attraction, and we gain an understanding that we need to know what we want, and we need to generate positive emotion around it, and we need to allow it. "Allowing" is the hardest part of this to grasp, and it is my feeling that allowance gets "cut off" by a hidden conversation that is running related to this feeling of *deserving* what we want.

And by the way, there is a difference between believing you deserve something "someday", and believing that you deserve it *right now,* the latter of which is absolutely the case.

You deserve it now. It is up to *you* to determine when you will actually allow it into your life.

Here is a process that will help you identify areas where you may actually feel less deserving than you want, or in some other way have "hidden" challenges related to having your desire fulfilled.

Think of one of your most passionate desires. One of the big ones that perhaps you have been thinking about for some time.

Now, let us say you closed your eyes, and fully visualized and got into the feeling of your desire fulfilled. What would it **mean** if when you opened your eyes, the desire had manifested right in front of you? Think about what your honest reaction would be.

Let us say it was a car. You close your eyes, visualize the car, feel what it would be like to be in that car driving along the open road, smelling the leather of the seats – all that stuff. Then you open your eyes, and your car is sitting there right in front of you.

You would probably freak out, wouldn't you? You would most likely be so incredibly frightened that you would run screaming! I mean think about it. Could you open your eyes, see a car before you that appeared out of thin air, and just sit calmly, feel wonderful, and thank the Universe for bringing your desire to you?

Doubtfully. And why is that?

Probably because it is just too big! But what defines something as "big" or "small" as it relates to a desire? It is determined by just how far out of your comfort zone it is. How far this item is outside what you consider to be your current parameters of reality.

You might feel as though you deserve the car...but do you feel that you deserve the ability to manifest it instantaneously? Probably not. And that comes from simply not understanding the true reason you are here. And if it is any consolation, just about nobody fully allows the true power which they have at their disposal. There are just far too many years and lifetimes of "learning" our limitations.

Do you feel you deserve good health now?

Do you feel you deserve a lean body now?

Do you feel you deserve abundance now?

Do you feel you deserve a happy marriage now?

The wording of these questions is important, because it is not an issue of whether or not you actually DO deserve something...because you most definitely DO. You deserve anything and everything you desire. You are this miracle of Creation for the express purpose of using this unique gift called Imagination to bring forth your desires into reality. Anything that stops you from feeling that you deserve your desires is based on false information, which can be unlearned. And once you do unlearn it, watch out! You will turn into a manifestation machine!

Next time anything at all happens to you that you do not enjoy, ask yourself if you truly believe that you deserve a *better* situation. However, you must understand that all of your circumstances are brought to you through the Law of Attraction, which states very clearly that "Energy attracts like Energy". You are literally vibrating a frequency that has brought this, and all other circumstances to you.

You do not have to believe it. Your belief in any of this has no effect on how the Law works. It will, however, have an effect on how the Law *occurs* for you.

Here is an easy way to gauge how "deserving" you truly feel at the deepest and most important levels:

Look around you. What do you see?

Whatever you are looking at is an indicator of what you feel you deserve. Nothing more, and nothing less.

Now, let me explain that.

"Deserving", the way most humans think about it, is an intellectual process of sorts. They figure that given everything they have said and done throughout their lives, they have "earned" (or they "deserve") to have a certain experience in their lives. They "deserve" to have a house that is x size, or a car that costs x amount of dollars, or a marriage that is x happy.

On the outside, they might look at their environment, and complain, "I can't believe this! I deserve so much more than this! This is not fair."

The tricky part to understand is that those statements are not reflective of your *true* beliefs. They may be intellectually sound, however. That is, you may work much harder than you are being compensated for. You may treat people a lot nicer than they treat you. You may be loyal to a spouse who does not return that courtesy. Therefore you figure that you "deserve" better, and that some cosmic injustice is being done.

While all that may be so, there are two things that are also true:

First, you are having the experience you are having because on some level, you are in vibrational resonance with it. You are magnetizing it.

Secondly, the reason you are vibrating the way you are, is that at your deepest levels, you do not really feel that you deserve any better (or worse) than you have right now. The reasons for that can run really deep, and are the kinds of things that are extracted through therapy and the like.

However, none of that really matters, because it has no bearing whatsoever on whether or not you are Deserving.

The proof that you Deserve anything you desire
is the fact that you Exist. Plain and simple.

Since most people do not understand that however, they have created this limiting system of Energy within themselves that they label as "being deserving only if...", and they literally hold themselves back from the exact experience they were put here to have.

This is something of an advanced concept. But to the extent that you can "get it", your manifesting skills will improve exponentially. Because when you truly know you deserve anything you want, there is literally nothing that is preventing it from coming your way.

Your Desires are Already Fulfilled

One of the toughest things for people to really integrate into their belief systems is that they **already have** everything they desire. They simply have to shift your awareness to it.

I know it seems like a lot to ask to believe. I mean our current situations sometimes feel so real and so permanent, that it is difficult to see that we can just "realize" something else. I mean, our desire certainly does not seem to exist "here", so where does it exist?

Well, it exists in our thoughts, and this should not be undervalued. We can see it in our minds eye. And if we do what we *should* when we have a desire for something, we also **feel** it with all of our senses, and focus our Imagination on the Emotion involved with having this desire fulfilled. When we do that, our desire has been brought into existence, and it is just waiting for us to become a part of it. We have assembled the Energy that is now pure potential to be an experience in our life. The problem is that so many of us do not consider our thoughts to be "real", but simply some non-existent imaginary image in our brain.

But the Energy that is your current experience of reality, and the Energy of the "thought" of your desire are simply vibrating on two totally different frequencies for you. Shift the Energy of your current awareness to the "other" frequency, and you will experience that as a reality. Because are not conscious of this, we just simply let our awareness follow the "easiest" path, based on its belief systems. We have programmed ourselves, or it has been programmed into us, to think and "do life" in this manner.

The fact is however, we can and *should* reclaim conscious control over our awareness. You now have all the steps you need - like deciding what your desires are, making lists, meditation – but are you taking action on them? If you are not, I can only assume it is because you just have not fully integrated the immense **possibility** that lies ahead when you begin to consciously create your life. And all it takes is a little more control over **the use of your imagination** – a gift for us, and a tool.

Imagination is **the** tool of creation, and it is free for us to use at any time. If we do not use it, life will seem totally out of our control, and our circumstances may appear as extremely grim, but it is all because that is what we believe. And remember your Ego is going to "support" you in this reality of yours with all kinds of logical reasons why you cannot change your circumstances in an instant. But it is all lies, yet it seems so easy to believe – and that is why so many believe it.

To reiterate: You DO have your desires now. Currently they seem to exist only in the domain of your imagination. But it is all just Energy. You are interpreting Energy in a certain way right now, and you have the ability to change your interpretation by creating a "replacement" reality in your imagination. But that is as far as many of us take it. We do not then "step in" to what we have created, because we have totally blocked out the knowledge that we know how to do that. But all knowledge is ours, if we claim it. We are just stuck in this loop of logic that tells us what is possible for us. But in fact, it is all possible. Right now.

If finding the time to explore all this is an issue, start by taking 5-10 minutes of time just to "be" with your desire. Bring it forth in your imagination, and surround it with nothing but positive feelings and emotions. In your minds eye, experience your desire on every sensory level – see it, hear it, touch it – and *in your vision*, think about how grateful you feel to be experiencing the desire right now. To the extent that you commit yourself to this, your desire absolutely has to come to you more quickly.

Your frequency will change to meet the frequency of your desire. Why? Because you are shifting your awareness to the experience of your desire on a regular basis. Your "Ego" is beginning to get the message, as you give it the experience of the positive feelings associated with your desire. Sooner or later the Ego says, "Hey, this new thing feels so much better than this current thing we have got going. Let's live in the new thing".

And then your awareness will begin to shift. But if you only *tease* your Ego with the experience of your desire - only taking time to visualize it as I described every now and then - then the Ego does not know you are serious, if that makes sense. It is going to cling to what is comfortable and "controllable" until it realizes that this new situation is going to make it even happier. I am not saying the Ego is in ultimate control, but when we first start with practicing these principles, it is one of the loudest voices we hear screaming that "it can't be done."

You are on a path to self-discovery. You are on your way to learning more about your purpose, and what is possible for you and all of humanity. This book is just another step in your path – and I believe that this knowledge that you create your experience, is some of the most important that you will attain. If you forget this ability, Life can be a series of struggles and battles.

Realize the Truth, and the Truth will set you Free.

How to "Be" Wealthy

When I first starting working very intentionally with the Law of Attraction, my wife and I went to see a 1.7 million dollar home that was for sale on a lake near where we currently lived. I do not want you to think that I am in any way making any personal statement about my current income or net worth…it is not at all the point of telling you this story, and as I type these words, we are not yet in the house I am going to describe. However, I will take great joy in updating you to the contrary!

Visiting this home was an incredible experience. Initially I think I approached this visit as an exercise in raising my wealth consciousness, because at that time, that 1.7 million was a dollar range that had my Ego wanting to scream!

I wanted to put myself in a place that had no evidence of lack whatsoever and just experience it…in a place that I knew already had a few of the features that I was looking for in "the ultimate home".

Now you need to know a few things. On my list of desires (and you DO have one of those, right?) at the top of the list is (and has been for years) a house on the lake. From there, I have been creating details like:

- Every room wired for audio
- A computer in the kitchen for recipe access
- Heated tile floors

- Multiple shower heads
- A nice dock
- Deep water for swimming
- A media room

You get the idea. Before I even saw the house, I had very specific "visions" if you will, of the view of the water from various rooms. One vision I had in particular was very clear. I was sitting in a chair in a long, hardwood floor room, a fireplace to my left, and a wall of arched windows in front of me with a view of the water. It was so vivid…I knew it was THE ROOM.

So you can imagine what must have gone through my head when I walked into this house for the first time, and in the living room was *exactly* what I had seen in my imagination before ever seeing it physically. I about fell over…and at the same time I knew that this was totally right.

Then, it continued from there. Every room had speakers for music. There was a heated tile floor in the bathroom and nine shower heads! They even had a small refrigerator in the master bath. Now I did not create the refrigerator in my vision, but knowing me, I probably would have eventually!

It had decks off every bedroom, perfect for entertaining just as I'd imagined. I love decks…and this house has decks galore! There was a beautiful dock in a cove of deep water, a view of the marina off in the distance, and great sunsets. The house was built by a builder for his personal use. He had intended to stay there for life. So you can imagine the attention to detail and quality that went into the construction of that home.

He even had a computer in the kitchen.

So what does this mean? I try not to jump to the interpretation that this is necessarily *my* house...or that it is coming right now. It *could* mean that, but it is not for me to decide that. I cannot force it, nor do I want to. I can only follow my intuition, pay attention to my ideas, and keep the vision alive.

Seeing this house really added some power to this whole experience of "being wealthy" because then I had something very real and specific to focus my creative Energy on (in an unattached way, of course). The house was no longer just a collection of concepts in my head. Now, I had seen it and touched it. I knew it existed in the physical. I just have to resist the urge to try to "figure out" how it is coming.

Clearly the Universe is in the process of delivering. The "coincidences" of this experience were absolutely ridiculous. One would have to be totally blind or at least very closed-minded not to see that. I mean it is almost as if the guy built this house 6 years ago to the spec sheet I just started creating a few months before I saw it.

So the message here for you is dream big, and dream specifically. This house showed up in our lives almost immediately after I began to meditate on what I wanted our "dream" home to be.

Go play with "being" wealthy. Shop for a home, a car, or *something* that connects you with the feeling of wealth. It really helps raise your vibration, and that is what you need. And, it is just fun to do!

Most importantly, **do not think about the money**. Shop as if paying for it is not even the issue. Go find what excites you! That does not mean to go spend a bunch of money if money is not currently a part of your experience, particularly if you are one who stresses over debt. Simply think about what you are going to end up with when you have it. Just remember that money is not always going to be the conduit to the "thing" in question.

Further, when you think about money, you are caught up in the "how" of the process and will then focus on trying to figure out ways the money will come, which is not your job. You just follow the signs and have the most fun possible.

This is a good point to talk about the "**This, or something better for the good of all concerned**" addendum you should place on all your desires. For example, if I get too attached to this particular house, I run the risk of missing an even *better* one charging its way toward me. You want to remain detached until the desire is ultimately fulfilled. That does not mean "do nothing". You *will* most likely be taking action, but take action as the Universe leads you, more than trying to forge the path yourself with intellectual thinking. Now if "planning it all out" feels totally natural, freeing, and just "right" to do, then perhaps that is your path. But if you have any stress or worry around forging your own path, that is not what you need to be doing.

So make a list and be detailed! If you do not, you are missing out, plain and simple. Writing them makes them even more real. Meditate on your list, and be on the lookout. Because the items you put your quality attention on, are coming now.

Who Wants to Be a Millionaire?

I know a lot of you are thinking "me!"...but I will almost bet that you are really thinking "I want to have a million dollars." These are not the same thing, though it certainly seems that they are at first. Doesn't the word "millionaire" imply that you have a million dollars?

Yes, that is exactly what it does. It IMPLIES you have a million dollars. I am sure there are people who call themselves millionaires who often have *more* than a million dollars – in the bank or whatever – and sometimes have *LESS*. But the distinction is this: Who they **are** – who they are **being** – is a millionaire. They will most likely always be a millionaire...that is, if they truly have developed Wealth Consciousness and thus naturally attract wealth through the Law of Attraction. It is unlikely that they will permanently lose their money, whereas a person who "clawed their way" to a million dollars, sacrificing everything, enduring long hours and no life to get there...has a much greater risk of losing everything, or a great deal of it because of what they associate with being a "millionaire". Not a lot of really positive things. Still they made their millions in spite of themselves – but how long will they hold it?

A *true* millionaire does not have to worry about losing everything. "Millionaire" has become a state of mind for them, not a number in a bank account. The feeling of being a millionaire - or someone who will always have plenty of money - is a very unique feeling. When I first started "trying it on", as I am going to suggest *you* do, it was a very powerful feeling. Not in terms of power over anything; it just sent a very significant surge through my being.

For seconds at a time, I would cross over into a true millionaire mindset, and every worry in my life, small and large, that had ANYTHING to do with money or the lack thereof, completely vanished. The feeling is indescribable. "Wealth" suddenly permeated all aspects of my being and I immediately felt so *light*. I also noticed that I immediately and significantly slowed down – just overall. It is as if my heart slowed, my thoughts slowed, my movement slowed. I simply was not in a hurry for anything.

I was able to savor the moment, because I had no concern with what I "needed to do", which had been almost always something related to acquiring money, or *needing* money to do something. It is amazing how money has an impact on so much in our lives in ways we never even think of regularly.

And when you can completely let go of any attachment to the need for money – when you can BE that you truly have unlimited resources and that money is simply not any kind of issue in your life – you suddenly realize just how much in your life money touches! It is a lot…and that is why so many people have such challenges around it…but *OH* when you can free yourself from it in that way!

In addition to the "slowing" of my overall pace, I also had a very marked psychological *and* physiological shift. I thought differently about so much. In the particular instance I am relating to you now, I was preparing dinner. I remember thinking, "We eat what we want, and have fun preparing it. This meal costs a lot of money, and it does not matter at all, because we can easily afford anything we want at any time." (Of course, I had that thought in a nanosecond, which sustained for several seconds.) It was just such an intensely freeing experience. And it was so powerful! I realized the concept of *being* Wealthy on a whole new level, and I could literally feel how magnetic I had become!

It far transcended affirmations like, "I have all the money I need for anything I want." **It was completely experiential,** and felt tremendously real, although like I said, at first I could only sustain it a few seconds. However I believe those few seconds were a TURBO-BOOST in the delivery of that reality.

Putting into words exactly what I do to achieve that state is proving very challenging, but I think the first logical step is to state the affirmation in your mind. But after that you have to "step into it". I cannot think of another way to put it. You just temporarily "forget" that anything other than that the essence of your affirmation IS the truth. Rather than focusing on "creating something new", simply forget about what you do not want to exist.

For example:

If your desire is to experience great wealth, but your predominant thoughts are on this "wealth" you *do not have* – even if you are trying to imagine yourself wealthy - you still have the whole "I do not yet have this" conversation running. And even though you are not necessarily conscious of it, the "I do not have it" vibration is a powerful attractive Energy – attracting more of the same for you. However, if you can – even temporarily – *forget* that you do not have the wealth you want, then your "wealthy" state sort of become the "de facto" state for you.

I know this is a tricky one. I wrestle with the language here as I am trying to describe something that is completely intangible and is much more linked to **feeling** than is possible to describe with words. It is about how strongly you can "play" with having your desire...and maybe the technique of forgetting might help you to experience that sense of "play" on a different level.

I can just tell you that I had been working a long time with "Being" wealthy by doing the wealthy things like shopping for homes and cars. However, it was an entirely different feeling to approach these things with the true *feeling* that I had plenty of money (or means) to get whatever I wanted. Knowing *how* I was going to *afford* what I wanted was not the issue at all, on any level. Not because I was thinking "The Universe *will* provide", but taking it a step further and saying, "**The Universe has already provided.**"

Many people believe that "being a millionaire" means being someone who will never have to worry about money again. We have got this idea that a million dollars is some kind of "magic number" with which all of our problems will be solved. And again, I would bet several "millionaires" would give you a thousand reasons that is not necessarily the case.

So, if you want to be a millionaire – or more accurately, someone who does not have to give money a second thought - be sure you play with the FEELINGS associated with BEING that. Do not think and try to feel "a million dollars". Think and feel how it will be to have *no concern with money whatsoever* – and hold that feeling as long as possible, as often as possible. Because that level of wealth could come with a lot less, or a lot more than a million dollars. Let the Universe decide the best and quickest way to provide.

When Those Around You Do Not Believe

So you have started integrating the scientific principles of the "Law of Attraction", or at least you are trying to, but your spouse, friends, or co-workers do not share your enthusiasm for this way of thinking. The big question I get is, "Will this affect the outcome of my efforts to manifest wealth?"

And the answer is that it totally depends on you. Now before I really get into that, let's back up and really look at your situation.

Remember that this spouse, these friends, these co-workers, or whomever it is that surrounds you and talks all of this down, are people that **you attracted into your life**. You first have to take responsibility for that. If you fight that basic truth, you are unlikely going to have success with these principles, because understanding that you attract EVERYTHING – pleasant or unpleasant – is the distinction that gives you the confidence to create anything you desire.

You cannot just say, "I attracted this great thing, but this other situation is someone else's fault entirely". And remember, that does not mean that you CREATED the situation. You have simply attracted it into your life either with conscious persistent thoughts, or unconscious thoughts and beliefs that run without you even taking much notice of them. This combination of thoughts creates your "vibration" which then attracts "like" vibrations.

When these people came into your life, you were most likely vibrating something very different than what you are starting to vibrate now. When you suddenly change "who you are", or work on raising your vibration to a new state, you are *going* to shake things up a bit among your sphere of influence. How can you not?

And you also have to remember that the path that you are on is *your* path. It is not for us to coerce others into our way of thinking or believing. And in fact, when we do that when they are not ready, we are only going to create conflict, which of course creates negative emotion, all of which simply begins to attract more of the same!

What makes this harder is that the people who are giving us a hard time about all this are coming from the mainstream view of what is "responsible". So we hear things like, "Yeah, well that all sounds great, but the bills need to be paid NOW and we have NO MONEY." If that sounds familiar to you, what is your first response when you hear this argument? Probably things along the lines of:

- They are right. This is goofy. What they are saying is perfectly logical.
- They do not know what they're missing. They are wrong. If they would just see it *my* way, we could change everything.
- They are making this so hard!

All of these are natural thought processes to have, given what we have been brought up to believe. But entertaining these thoughts from others is sure to do nothing but immediately lower your vibrations and attract more of *their* version of reality than the one you are creating.

So what do you do? Is their Energy affecting the outcome of what you are trying to create?

If you allow their thoughts to dominate your emotions, then they absolutely will have an impact. And you also have to remember that they are not "wrong", per se...and certainly not in their own minds. Their belief systems are firmly entrenched, and if they hear something they interpret to be "pie in the sky", they are not simply going to flip-flop into a new belief system because it "sounds good". And in fact, the fact that it sounds so good is likely to repel them.

But what if you gave them absolute freedom to feel however they want about this, and in no way attach their thoughts to your own emotions? After all, it is *you* who is being "unreasonable" here by society's definition. You are changing the rules of who you are and what you believe is possible in midstream. You have got to give the rest of the world time to catch up, and a *reason* to join you, if that is what you want them to do.

You see, if you are being challenged by a spouse or friend, you have 3 choices.

1. You can bend to their emotional responses and slow or give up completely on your journey into attracting the life you desire.

2. You can choose to no longer associate yourself with them if you find yourself unable to pursue who you truly are with them in your life. I acknowledge that this is a pretty harsh step, and I more highly recommend the *next* choice.
3. Commit yourself to creating a vision for **your** future. If you want your spouse, friends, or co-workers to be a part of that vision, then put them there. Focus on the feelings associated with having those you care about taking this incredible journey with you.

Do not focus on *changing* them, because not only is that not your "job", but it is only a STEP TOWARD what you really want...and you should always "leap frog" those interim steps when creating your vision, because again, you are trying to determine HOW your desire will be fulfilled when it is not up to you at all!

The third choice is a "lead by example" choice. Your only responsibility is to implement these principles into your own life wherever you can, and let those you care about watch what happens.

This more subtle approach will allow you to enter into conversation about what you are doing much more lightly.

In the meantime, just keep the peace. Do not try to rationalize with someone who is in a panic about money that the Universe will provide if they just raise their vibrations. That probably will not have the impact you are looking for.

Using the Law of Attraction to attain wealth does not mean to throw away responsibility. After all, if you do things you feel in your heart are irresponsible in the name of "proving your faith in the system", eventually, your intellect will get the best of you. At a core level you do not really feel good about being irresponsible. Plus, irresponsible behavior makes it even more difficult to get those around us to accept these principles as being valid.

So again...lead by example...and do it quietly and peacefully. Eventually, if it is meant to be, those close to you will follow. And if it is clear that they will only continue to work to impede your personal growth through negativity, doubt, and fear, then you have to make some serious choices, or restructure your vision to include more harmonious relationships with these people.

Meeting Abraham

I have included this information in the "Technical Support" section, because an important aspect of what I am going to share with you was a "block" for me for a long time.

There are many of you who know all about Abraham and Jerry and Esther Hicks. I know this, because I have heard from many students that much of the Wealth Beyond Reason material reminds them of the Abraham material. I have been asked for years whether I am familiar with the Abraham teachings, and because of those questions, I *was* familiar with them, and finally I felt that it was time for me to explore the material further.

If you are already familiar with Abraham, bear with me for a minute. If not, I will explain why I previously never really gave the material too much of my time.

You see, Abraham is a group of non-physical teachers who are channeled through Esther Hicks.

Now, for several of you, sirens are going off! "Channeled? Excuse me? I thought we were talking scientifically here, Bob. What are you on about?"

And those were my thoughts exactly, when I first heard about the material. I had a pre-judgment, if you will, about "channeling". But actually, I had absolutely **no knowledge on the subject whatsoever**, so I was easily led by the mainstream thinking from which I most definitely came, and therefore channeling was a concept that I just could not get my logical mind to accept fully.

If it had not been for David Cameron (author of "A Happy Pocket Full of Money") asking me if I had ever looked into channeling, I might not be writing about Abraham now, and I would not be having the rapid-fire succession of breakthroughs in manifestation that I am having even as I type this!

Actually, I was a little surprised when David asked me about it, since his material was so "scientific". He told me that learning to channel would actually help me to become a better teacher – and I was just thinking "Ohhhhhh, kay". And for a while, I did nothing about it. But then, as will happen when the Universe works to fulfill your *true* desires, the subject of channeling appeared *everywhere* in my life. I had several other students asking me more about Abraham-Hicks, and other channeled material. So finally I just thought "Ok, already! I'll look into it!!"

Long story short, channeling is truly not the "mystical" stuff I always thought, and in fact, is just as scientific as any of the other material discussed in the program. It is fully explainable and yes, even *logical*, once you allow yourself to be open to the information.

Now I already know that there are some among you that will most likely *never* accept channeling as an appropriate practice, and I am not asking you to. In fact, I am not even asking you to believe in it at all, because it simply does not matter. What I would ask, is that you would evaluate information that is "channeled", just as you would any other material that you read or listen to. Does it resonate with you? Does it uplift you? Give you hope? Does it help you in any way? Then what difference does it make where it came from?

Once I was more open to the subject of channeling, I felt more ready to explore the Abraham material. After all, I knew it had helped thousands and thousands of people to become more deliberate creators. I knew that many "Wealth Beyond Reason" students absolutely adored the material. And suddenly I felt much more open to receiving whatever wisdom there was to receive. I knew Abraham taught on the same subjects we teach in Wealth Beyond Reason, and given that I am always looking for new distinctions, what logic was there in resisting the material? Absolutely none.

So, I did what I am going to suggest you do. I visited the Abraham-Hicks web site:

http://www.abraham-hicks.com

and I listened to their free introductory material. And by the way, they have a *lot* of free material. You could read for days over there! I am not going to regurgitate any of the material here, because you can read it yourself. It is sufficient to note that we are all in agreement that the Law of Attraction is the dominate creative force in the Universe, we are all utilizing it all the time, whether or not we are doing it on purpose, and that raising your vibration – or feeling good – is the key to making it work for you.

After listening to the introductory material, I ordered what they call their starter set, because it contains a lot of great information, and is a great value. After receiving that and listening to it, there was this great new sense of "coming home". It is hard to explain, but it was everything I wanted to hear...and I kept thinking as I was listening how it directly addressed not only my own questions, but questions I get from many "Wealth Beyond Reason" students as well. Eight hundred seminars suddenly wrote themselves in my head, and I felt myself going into overload! But the big kicker was that as I went back to the web site to explore a little more, I noticed that their next live workshop was going to be held here in Atlanta, only three days after I had received their tapes in the mail.

Coincidence? Please!

Their schedule has them all over the country all year and ONE time in Atlanta, the very week I got their material. Making the decision to go was a complete no-brainer.

The purpose of this chapter is not to tell you everything I learned there. That would be impractical, since it was an all day event, plus so much of what you "get" from an experience like that defies description. But basically, the format is that once Esther Hicks begins to channel the material, they speak for about 30 minutes or so, and the audience members then ask Abraham questions. There is no question that is off limits. I had some things in mind that I would have asked but virtually every point in my mind was addressed eventually through someone else's asking, or was answered in my own mind nearly immediately upon considering the question.

The message of Abraham is clear: Find something to be happy about. That is it. But we all just *insist* on finding things to *fix* or to *worry* about – feeling certain that we must *DO* something, or *work* for those things that we want. If there is one thing that I got very powerfully during that weekend, it is just how false that is. And the freedom you will feel when you fully understand it is indescribable.

I see so many people still trying to figure out how the Universe will deliver their desires, when it is absolutely not their job.

Our job is to discover what we want, and bask in joy wherever we can find it. We do not have to dwell on what we want. The Universe knows, as long as we are clear. That is why we make our lists, or put pictures in a box, or make a collage, or whatever we do to make our desires more "real". Then, we simply have to allow it…and we do that by staying in a place where your vibration matches what we want. We absolutely can not do that if we worry, stress, and argue that our current situation is "reality", because we will absolutely get more of whatever our dominant thought is.

I also learned that there are NO limitations to having what you want, except to the extent that you believe, or feel, and vibrate that there are. And you can kick and scream and insist that YOUR situation is different, and thus is will be, and there is nothing that anyone can do about it…because **no one can vibrate for anyone else**! That is important to know. You cannot FIX anyone else, nor should you try. Sympathizing with someone, or feeling their pain, serves neither of you. For you to lower your vibration only takes away from your personal experience, and contributes more low vibrations to the experience of the person you are trying to help.

Your job is to take care of *you*, and to inspire by example. And when people call you "selfish", understand that selfish is not a bad thing.

Your life is about YOUR LIFE...and living it with JOY! It is all about Joy in the moment, every moment! It is the secret to having everything you want quickly! And, while it may seem selfish, you are actually putting yourself in the position of helping more people than you can possibly imagine, because you will be contributing maximum value to the world when you live the life you are designed to live.

So if the message is so simple, why are their hundreds of books, tapes, CDs, teachers, and products? **Because we as humans are just stubborn and resistant to change**. That is it! We just have a hard time allowing!

I tell you this with such fervor because as a result of reading the Abraham-Hicks material, I have had a tremendous shift! But, having said that, I could not have "heard" Abraham without having gone down the more scientific path I have traveled. That may be so with you as well. I have heard from many students that they have studied Abraham for years, but the "Wealth Beyond Reason" material gave them a new grasp of it, and obviously I am joyous as a result of knowing that! I was not ready to hear Abraham's message until certain other distinctions had been made in ways that my logical, analytical, and skeptical mind would have accepted. But I am abundantly thankful that I have come back to this work in exactly the way that I have. It is why I am inviting you to look at it yourself. Maybe you will embrace it now. Maybe later. Maybe not at all. But it is entirely too powerful not to share with you.

In the "Resources" section of this book, I have also pointed toward a site that offers a free electronic book called the "Have A Nice Day Workbook" which is a compilation of Abraham teachings in a handbook form. If you feel at all led, please download it and do the work. Again, I might not have felt led to do it at all, had I not familiarized myself with the Abraham material through the starter CDs or the workshop, so I really have no idea how you will be led to act. I have provided a link to it all the same, and I personally am delighted in what is provided.

In any case, it is my sincere desire that you find something – *anything* - to be happy about.

It is why you are here.

Attraction vs. Creation

There is a distinction that can be made between **Attracting** reality and **Creating** it. And while at a quantum level, There really isn't any difference, I think that at a human intellectual level, there is a way of looking at attracting and creating so that you can more easily accept that you have these abilities.

By now you understand on some level that **we are Energy**, vibrating at a certain frequency. Our reality is a direct result of what we are vibrating. Our thoughts cause our vibration, and we attract "like vibrations" – we literally magnetize our desires into our lives. But are we creating them from thin air, or something else?

On one level, I have to say we *are* creating them from thin air. Nothing really exists in our reality without us observing it. This is a basic truth of quantum physics. But some people just have a hard time grasping that, or knowing what to do with it exactly. Still, if we can gain an acceptance that we attract our desires through some kind of "logical scientific process", we can move more rapidly through the work. We really need to clear out any blockages however we can so we are free to dream big without restriction.

People look at their circumstances and think, "Did I create this? Did I create this house? Did I create hunger in the world? Did I create this woman I married (or man)? I mean how could I create **everything**? How could I create high-definition television when I know nothing about electronics? Obviously, somebody else is doing something!"

Yes. We are all out here, creating and attracting our own realities. We are vibrating certain thoughts out into the Universe, some of them way below the conscious level, and as a result of our vibrations, we are attracting **like Energy** into our experience. This Energy could have originated somewhere else completely. We will meet, or come into contact with, other people or situations that are sending out a vibration that our vibration attracts.

So you are brought to a particularly unpleasant person by some means...or you hear something on the news that sounds terrible – something you would never create on purpose – and, this happens because it is attracted to whatever you are vibrating. That does not mean that you *created* whatever that "bad thing" was on the news. It simply means that whatever it is that you are vibrating at this moment allows that news to enter your life in some way.

It is not like you consciously created a horrible train derailment or something. But some combination of Energy did, and for whatever reason, your vibration attracted that experience into your life at a level deeper than you are conscious of.

This is why what we vibrate is so important. By the way, I acknowledge that vibrate is a funny word. It conjures up all kinds of images that can cause a giggle, but there is really no other way to say it. We are vibrating at *some* frequency that magnetizes other Energy just like it. And we change our vibrations with our thoughts. So what are we thinking? I mean *really thinking and feeling* the deepest level?

You have had the experience of thinking of someone, and suddenly they call, or you will think of something you need - an item like a pair of scissors or something – and BING, there they are in front of you. You can "rationalize" why they are there. It is not as if to your conscious mind they were not there, and then you suddenly materialized them. But actually, that IS what you are doing at a quantum level.

Why can things like scissors manifest nearly instantly, and other things that you are really putting your attention on - like a new house, car, or relationship - seem to take forever? Well, the details are going to be different for everyone, but *it is always about what you are vibrating.*

It could be that you are just too attached to these bigger things. You are putting SO much attention into it, that you are giving the Ego a LOT to work with, distort, and try to convince you is impossible. So just be aware of that.

The potential here, once you really get a handle on controlling more aspects of your vibration, is **instant manifestation**. Wizardry, if you will. Do I believe that is possible? Absolutely, 100%.

Put yourself into the thoughts and feelings of your desire fulfilled every day. This is different from simply "remembering" what you want. This is about having the experience that your desires are a part of your reality, today!

The Experiential Meditation at the end of this book is great for helping you do that. You will get into a highly focused vibration that will attract what you meditate on into your life. As often as you can do this, do it. It will accelerate the change in your life, absolutely.

I want to share one distinction with you in hopes that it would give you another way to look at how all of this works, and just what we are creating directly, and what we have attracted by accident. Those "accidental manifestations" are those things that have no apparent logic as to why they are there. Still, you must understand that it is *perfect* that they are there.

You should be thankful beyond belief that they ARE there, because they exist for you because you have this incredible ability to design your life with your thoughts. All you have to do is work on cleaning up those thoughts – do it *on purpose* and take control - and you can design the life of your absolute, most passionate and exciting dreams!

Raising Your Vibration

How to become more magnetic

Raising your vibration really comes down to one thing: **Find something to be truly happy about**. Often, however, that is easier said than done. If you are in a situation that reminds you of "how things are", rather than how you would really like them to be, it is often difficult to switch emotional gears. Still, it must be done! Otherwise, you will always attract more experiences that will keep you in the negative space, until you either purposefully distract yourself, or something else distracts you.

The following is a very short list of ways that you can raise your vibration in a positive way. If you have created your list of things that you truly desire, and are clear on why you want them, then maintaining a high vibrational state will cause them to come to you more swiftly. When you feel yourself being pulled in a negative emotional direction, refer to this list for ideas of activities you can undertake that will shift your awareness to more positive things. These are just a very few suggestions of the countless available to you!

1. Take a walk.

2. See a funny movie.

3. Call or visit a friend.

4. Play a video game.

5. Read an uplifting or motivational book.

6. Play with a pet.

7. Do some gardening. (Anything involving nature is a wonderful idea, as you will be constantly reminded of the abundance and effortlessness of the Universe to create magnificent things!)

8. Listen to your favorite music.

9. Meditate.

10. Listen to a comedy tape or CD (or even an album, if you have any of those old things).

11. Smile. Even if you have to force it at first.

12. Add more items to your list of desires. This is a great one. Nothing raises your vibration quite like getting all excited about getting new stuff!

13. Go shopping for more ideas of things you want. You do not have to buy anything, but creating the parameters of your new reality this way can be very exciting!

14. Allow yourself time to spend with your hobby or hobbies.

15. Eat "living" foods. While this is a topic for another whole book, the benefits of eating living foods is enormous. One terrific side benefit aside from the numerous health aspects of this way of eating is a rise in your vibration and overall Energy level. Try an ounce of wheatgrass juice from time to time (if you can tolerate the flavor).

16. **Exercise.** This one is so important, I could write another book on it (and I might). Exercising helps you on so many levels. It raises your Energy level by raising your metabolism. This alone is a "vibration-raising" benefit.

But the benefits of exercise extend beyond the physical. When you are exercising, you simply *feel* better about yourself on an emotional level. You know you are doing something that prolongs your life and health. You tend to like the way you look more. All of these things make you *feel good.*

If, however, you feel sluggish and lethargic due to inactivity, or you look in the mirror first thing in the morning and say "Yuck", you begin a downward spiral into negative feelings. At best, you run a continuous program of ill-feelings that will absolutely lower your level of magnetism to those things you want the most.

If you want some inspiration in this area, I highly recommend you check out one of the other "Boundless Living" websites, called BodyChangers. If the stories at that site do not motivate you to exercise and take control over the physical aspect of who you are, then I honestly do not know what will:

http://www.bodychangers.com

Are You Feeling Stuck?

Sometimes when you start using these principles to create wealth, you can experience some frustration because things are not moving along the way you would like. I have heard from some folks who say, "I have been working with these principles for weeks now, and things just aren't happening. In fact, they seem worse now than before."

If the latter is true, you can be sure of one thing: Something *is* happening. You have started to become an active participant in your life. You have started *designing* your life, and the Universe is responding. Now, sometimes what occurs is not what you would expect or *want* at the moment, but the infinite intelligence of the Universe has decided that whatever is occurring for you is the most efficient way to deliver on what you are really putting out there.

Consider carefully the following things that can absolutely slow you down as you begin to consciously attract Wealth into your life. Be honest with yourself here.

Have you made your list of desires? I know a lot of people read through material like this and keep all the work in their head. They read that they are to make a list, but they just never get around to it, or they think that keeping it in their head is enough. Perhaps it is, but it will also slow you down. Writing brings your desire to another level of reality, and it helps you to better solidify what you really want. This brings us to the next point:

Are you asking for what you really want, or are you asking for the MEANS for getting what you want? Are you asking for the house on the lake, or are you asking for the *money* to buy for the house on the lake. Money is a means to an end, and not what you should be asking for at all. Money, you will remember is not even real. It is a symbol of wealth – a medium for exchange – and nothing more. Money has no value unless it is being used. So asking for money is asking for nothing. Ask for what you want.

Now, you may find that money comes to you as a result of asking for that house on the lake. Or you might get that house on the lake by an unexpected means. But if you do not ask for what you *really* want, you are only delaying receiving it.

There is another level to this. Perhaps you ask for what you want, and then start looking for it to manifest in a specific way. For example, you ask for the Mercedes, and then you do nothing but buy lottery tickets expecting that this is **the** way you will get it. Or, you start looking for an increase in your business as **the** way you are going to get the **money** to get the car. So you are putting all your focus on something 3 steps away from your actual desire. You *must* stop doing that.

Are you having fun? Or have you made "creating your wealth" using these principles a **JOB**? It is **not** a job, and it should not *feel* like one. You are completely defeating the purpose of all of this if it feels like work.

Approaching this with the attitude that it is work, or a chore, does nothing but lower your vibration and wrap the whole process up in a layer of "yuck". The Universe does not try to figure out what you "really mean", so you do not get what you are saying that you want. The law of attraction simply works to attract more feeling of "yuck", or the feeling that this is a lot of hard work.

You attract what you think about or vibrate. RELAX for crying out loud! Make your list, feel the experience of having it (and this should feel wonderful – not stressful), and the just LET IT GO! Go have fun. Do not **dwell** on all this!

Are you putting a timetable on your manifestation? Of course, you want your desires to be fulfilled immediately. But for most of us, our belief system does not support this. So you want something **now** and yet you actively do not believe it will happen **now**, so it does not happen **now**. And although you have this idea that it *should* happen **now**, you do not believe it will happen **now**, so it never comes…because **"now"** is all there really is. Does that make sense?

Do not worry about the timetable. Seriously. Your Ego demands results now, but *impatience* really causes you nothing but trouble, and will keep you exactly where you are now. The Ego wants to stay in control.

Things will come to you at the perfect time, to the extent that you allow them.

You have to remember that you are living a very human experience right now, and depending on your background, this process of allowing yourself to have whatever you want can be fairly challenging. But your Body – this physical experience – is just one small fraction of who you really are – the Source of you – which is really just part of the ONE – God, the Universe – which has NO inherit limitations whatsoever. Your Ego – this annoying little thought process – is keeping you small and limited, but only because you allow that. Simply decide not to allow that any longer.

Another thing that slows people down is **not taking action** on going out and **being** Wealthy, as discussed in the "How to 'Be' Wealthy" section of this book.

Go look at luxury homes. Go test drive the Mercedes. Do all that fun stuff. Please do not be one of those people just reading these words and saying, "uh huh, yeah, okay I'll get around to doing that." but then never doing it. Surely you do not expect results from that, do you?

Another area people get stuck is in their "Giving".

I hear from some people who say, "I have tithed, I have given, and I have seen nothing." Here's the truth: You have either gotten your return and not recognized it because you are looking for it in a certain way, OR you have got an active *lack of belief* that it will flow to you as a result of giving. Plain and simple. You can argue with me all day on that one, but if you will take a step back and be honest with yourself, you will see that it is true.

I want nothing more than for you to have *unreasonable* success with this material. But please remember that this is to be a **fun, joyous experience**. That can be challenging sometimes if your situation seems desperate, but you have to be light about this.

And remember that sometimes, it is going to require something of a "breakdown" before the Universe can deliver what you truly want.

A lot of people ask for something different in their lives, and then totally freak out when change actually starts to occur! **Welcome the change**, no matter how frantically your Ego or intellect tries to convince you that you are one step away from total ruin. If you have got your eye firmly on the prize, the Universe will not ultimately let you down.

Creating With a Clean Slate

I want to talk about what I believe to be one of the biggest "slow-downs" you will run up against when you begin to purposefully use the Law of Attraction in your life. It comes from just a slight misinterpretation of one of the first steps in the process, which is deciding what you do not want, and then using that as a springboard to getting clarity about what you DO want.

Oftentimes, we will identify a situation that we clearly do not want and make the decision that we want a *different version* of it, instead of **something else entirely**. Hear that again: You know you do not want something like a job or a relationship, and you say to yourself, "Well, I'd like this job or relationship to be *this* way instead."

Now think about what you have done. You are requesting that something outside of you that already exists, *change* to your liking. Well, what if it does not WANT to be changed? If you are in a relationship, and it is not going to the way you want it to, you might say, "Well, I want him or her to be THIS way in this relationship." Well guess what? You cannot vibrate for them! You cannot change them.

However, you *can* attract something totally new and totally fulfilling. And before I go on to how you do that, remember this: If you are trying to change something, you will, by default, have some amount of Energy on what is WRONG with it, adding more Energy to what you are trying to change or eliminate.

I gained a very powerful distinction from reading a book called "Merlin's Message" by Marelin Thornton (see our "Resources" section) which was that as creators, it serves us much better to **start with a clean slate.**

Close your eyes and just pretend you are starting completely over with your Reality. You have a totally blank palette onto which you can paint anything you want. Of course, you are free to paint those things in your life that you already have that bring you great joy, but there is absolutely no necessity to include *any* version of the things that do *not* bring you joy.

Now in some cases that might not be too easy, especially if it is **people in your life** with whom you have a long history, but with whom you are no longer growing productively. However, your attachment to *anything* out of sense of guilt, or responsibility, or whatever your Ego says you "should" feel about something, does not serve you or the person or situation in question.

For example, let's say you start this process in the way I am going to suggest in just a minute. Pretend you have nothing, and know no one, just for the purposes of this exercise, and that you are about to **create everything and everyone** that you wish to be a part of your experience! ·

You start with your eyes closed, looking at this clean slate – Infinite Possibility. Now you start creating your reality from the ground up. Where do you want to be? I am not talking about your house. I am talking about your geographic location.

The country? The city? Surrounded by mountains? On a lake?

Create that picture.

What is the temperature? Cool? Warm? Is there a breeze? Feel it – and smell it.

Now start to create your home. If you do not know where to start, just gently ask the question: "What would my perfect home be like?" Trust me, your higher self knows exactly what that would be. Just allow any feelings or images to come in. Pay particular attention to the feelings, and think about the essence of what you would like your home to give to you.

Freedom? Security? Peace? Let the feelings guide the creation of your images. Begin to add furniture, accessories – **whatever you want**.

Then you might create your prosperity level. How wealthy do you want to be? And more importantly, what would that level of wealth **feel** like? That is, what **core desire** would having that kind of wealth fulfill, and then what would that **feel like**? You can ask no more important question!

After you have had some fun creating your home and living environment, you can add the relationships you would like to have. There is really no specific order to all of this. I am just giving you an example of the process to give you an idea.

I want you to see the BIG PICTURE here. **You can have whatever you want**. That does not simply mean you can have "reasonable versions" of what you already have, or that you can "figure out" how you could get.

It means, **whatever you can imagine can be yours**. But you have to give yourself the freedom to paint that picture exactly how you want it, rather than how you think *others* would feel appropriate for you to paint it.

One of the best ways to do that is to put yourself in the place – even if just for a few minutes at a time – that there IS nothing else other than that you are creating. You are starting completely from scratch.

Again, you can certainly choose things from your current reality to remain there, but do not use them as a starting point from which to "modify" your reality. Add them in, one at a time, only as you are sure that their presence in your reality will provide you with boundless joy and the freedom to be who you are and do exactly what you want to do to express yourself fully in your life experience! That is what this life is all about.

Meditation is a perfect time to do this. Tapping into Source through meditation and creating that clean slate is a wonderful way to begin to magnetize what you **really** want. Of course, you want to be very much in touch with the *reasons* you want these things – and how they will make you feel. You will want to experience those feelings as fully as possible.

The basic idea here is to not limit yourself in the least. I believe my friend Joe Vitale (author of "Spiritual Marketing", which is part of the "Wealth Beyond Reason" online program) once wrote a great piece called "*How to Think Like God*". It's a huge concept, but when we are designing our lives, we do have that kind of creative power...and **if we were God, what would we create?**

Do you think that God would think small in any way? Do you think God would compromise? Do you think God would settle, or worry about what others would think?

Well, neither then, should you.

Have You Forgotten How to Play?

You know just about everything you read regarding the Law of Attraction stresses the importance of having FUN with this process of attracting wealth and your other desires. Of course, we now know that there is a very scientific reason for that! At a Quantum Level, our Energy is simply more attractive to the like Energy of our desire fulfilled when we are at high emotion, rather than low.

Remember that high emotion can feel good or bad, but having *fun* assures that you will be thinking more positively in general about the things you want in your life, rather than those things you do not.

But a lot of us, when it comes right down to it, just have a really hard time having fun with this process. We are so serious about it. We are taking it on like we do all the areas of our lives, which by the way, is what got us to the very state we want to change!

I get a lot of questions from folks like, "Am I doing this right? Am I phrasing this right?", and while I certainly understand the need for clarification on certain points, I detect with some of these people that this is just another *chore* on their list of things to do, albeit a slightly more interesting one.

I am not suggesting that people are *suffering* over learning the principles (though I know that some are, unfortunately), but there is a definite LACK of play as well. And I truly think many of us have forgotten how, or never really *learned* to play! To just delight in absolutely letting go of "composure" or your serious tone, and just let loose!

It is one of the things I personally deal with the most. Even knowing what I know, and making the changes that I have to this point using the Law of Attraction, I still catch myself taking the process very seriously at times.

I am sure we do this because we are sometimes dealing with some very "serious" issues, related to why we are taking on this education in the first place. Perhaps someone is ill, or you think you desperately need money or something along those lines. It is hard to let go of your awareness of that so-called *evidence*, long enough to actually have **fun** – real exuberant, physically buzzing FUN – imagining something different! Something better. Something that *is* whatever you WANT it to be!

I have always taken things seriously (some people tell me it's because I'm a Libra – whatever that means). Even way back in my very early years I remember being embroiled in self-imposed drama, at school and at home. That pattern followed me through my high school years in a huge way, until finally my first year of college, I really saw what I had become, and started a total shift in the other direction…a journey I am still taking.

From time to time, I do have a hard time loosening up, or being fully self-expressed. I am only telling you this because I am pretty sure there are a lot of us out there. And what I am telling you is this: If you do not learn to PLAY with these principles….if you cannot *lighten up…* you should probably expect more of what you have currently got, or for things to get worse. Because without knowing it, you are attaching an Energy that is associated with the unpleasant feeling of "working so hard with these principles and hoping upon hope that they're really true". So a *freeing fulfillment of your desire associated with joy* is the *last* thing you are actually attracting.

Unfortunately many are really uptight about Play. They are afraid of feeling or appearing irresponsible, or they have a lack of self-confidence that has them thinking that people will judge them in a state of play. A perfect example of this is men who will not dance. These guys generally do not dance because they feel they *cannot* dance, so why would they go out and make idiots of themselves, only to be judged by others?

Gee, I wonder how I know all this?

The worst part is there is often a *yearning* associated with this feeling. A *wishing* that you *could* be more self-expressed, free of the opinions of others. You have a desire to go make an idiot of yourself if you want to, because what you are doing is fun to YOU and who cares what others think? And of course! It is our natural state! We have a core desire to be fully expressed, and so many are *painfully* non-expressed, and their desires simply cannot flow to them!

So how do you change that? How can you just "loosen up" suddenly, and change a part of who you have been being for so many years that it is who you actually think you are?

It is just like anything else! **You attract it!** Along with seeing yourself in the new car or house, **see yourself being a playful free spirit**, who attracts fun all the time! Imagine what you will feel like when you feel free to play! *How* will you play? When whatever is holding you back from playing now is no longer an issue (like other people's thoughts of you or whatever), what will you do?

Spend time visualizing that, and most importantly FEELING that. You will find that the Universe will start presenting you with either more opportunities to play, like parties or something, or you will just begin to experience an unexplainable shift in your being. A lightness. Bask in those opportunities! And when you find yourself in the height of your play, take a moment to be with your other desires!

Take advantage of the fact that you are in a highly magnetic state, and really feel your *other* desires too...the car, the house, health, or whatever! This is why play is so important. It *keeps* you in a highly magnetic positive state, and ultimately that is what we want!

So if you are feeling a little frustrated with this whole process, it is assuredly because you are not playing with it. You are "taking it on", or you are "working on it", and that is not really what your Soul wants, I assure you. I am assuming that Play is the end result you are looking for in all of this.

After all, what are you going to do with all your wealth, if not Play? However, do not expect something magical to occur once you get all the wealth and are assumedly ready to play! If you have not learned to play your entire life, what makes you think you will suddenly know how once you obtain the wealth to live that life?

I will tell you again, you have to *create* the Play in your life if it is not currently there. **When you are imagining your desires, imagine yourself ENJOYING Them**! PLAYING in them! Because if you are not playing with this, then you are visualizing your dream fulfilled, but with this "serious tone" about everything...so when you DO finally realize this vision, how are you going to feel about it? SERIOUS! THAT is what you created!

You will find yourself in your brand new house, filled with a bunch of *serious thoughts* like, "How can I maintain this?" or "What's next? ...Gotta keep working on something." Create ALL aspects of your future...not just that it exists! Also create how it *feels* to you that it exists.

You should be doing this anyway, of course. But what are you really feeling? I am sure there is a whole "Wow, this will be great when it happens feeling", but look carefully behind that to make sure there is not another conversation running like, "I have been working on this vision for so long. Where is it? What am I doing wrong? I am going to have to *blah blah blah* harder to make this happen!" It is totally natural to have that conversation going, but maybe if you are aware of it, you can stop it quickly.

We are here to play! So if you are not playing now and do not even feel like you know *how*, imagine that you do! Or ask the Universe to show you how to play! Then just listen for the answer. It really is that simple!

How to Recognize the Signs

When you begin to practice these techniques of attracting your reality, financial or otherwise, you are going to be looking for (and hopefully following) *signs* that appear to lead you in the right direction.

People or things will suddenly show up in your life for no logical reason. You will start hearing about certain job offers, or similar things that are fairly obvious to those even paying peripheral attention.

But if those are the *only* types of signs you are looking for, you are probably missing out on numerous opportunities to accelerate the realization of your desire. One of the places you should probably look the hardest is when you are sure something is *not* a sign. If you EVER hear yourself thinking "coincidence", start thinking "sign" instead.

Also, sometimes we seem to get "signs" that things are going completely opposite of the way that we want. But consider that the event that you think is so terrible -that you think is the opposite of what you want - is also very likely to be a sign. It also might be an awakening that perhaps you did not create a "big picture" in terms of your desire.

Here's an example. Let's assume that one of your strong desires is that you are out of your current house and in that house on the lake. The house on the lake is obviously a symbol of prosperity for you, and yet somehow you suddenly start taking financial hit after hit. You suddenly do not have money to pay your bills. All the while you are desperately thinking "House on the Lake, House on the Lake", and the situation seems to accelerate in the WRONG direction.

Finally you can not pay your mortgage and you lose the house you are living in.

This is something of an extreme example, but what happened there?

Well, you **fulfilled** the first part of your desire to be out of the house you were currently in. Given your belief system, or level of Wealth Consciousness, this might have been the most "efficient" way for the Universe to get you out of the house. Perhaps you never would have ended up in a house on the lake if you hadn't been "forced" to make a change. And there could be a lot of reasons for that. You might have an inner belief that while you like dreaming about the house on the lake, you are really comfortable where you are, and it would take a lot for you to actually take action towards that house on the lake. So to facilitate the desire that you just KEPT affirming to yourself, the Universe took whatever action would facilitate you FIRST getting out of the current house.

Of course, it could have played out an infinite number of ways, but it is going to depend on your level of Wealth Consciousness. What sequence of events would your current belief system allow to be unfolded in front of you? You can start to see just how important it is to really get this stuff on a deep level. Ironic, because what we are really working **so hard** to do now, it to simply return to our **true nature**. That is how far we have strayed from the path. But the path is right there in front of us, should we just choose to follow it.

So be very careful when you formulate your visions that you add the statement "**for the good of all concerned**"...and "**I have all this or even better**". These statements allow the Universe some flexibility, and ultimately you win by not attempting to direct the Universe laws in the process of delivery. If you see that the fulfillment of your desire is not happening, or something very undesirable is going, go back and really look at how you have put your desire together in your imagination. Are there some built-in "implications" that may not be what you would write down your desire to be, but are sort of "givens" deep in your mind. Those are all attracting too.

You might think, "Man, that Universe is a picky son of a gun!" But really, it is not. It is the most perfect reality creation fulfillment mechanism that could possibly exist. It gives you more of exactly what you put into it. You just have to get extremely clear on what you are putting in.

So when it comes to "signs", and how to look for them, just know they are everywhere, and sometimes seem so small and insignificant.

So look at everything, but do not obsess over it. Enjoy what pops up for you, and follow your intuition all along the way.

As you get better at all this, it will not be such constant "work" to keep your head on straight. Your belief systems will shift, and it will become natural. But when you think you see a sign, and you do not know what to do about it, just be still and ask yourself, "What do I *want* to do about it?" and then act upon that answer.

Ideas are Energy

...and you have them for a reason

Did you ever have the experience of seeing a movie that you had the idea for, or something very similar? Did you ever think of an invention and then a year or so later, your exact invention comes out, created by someone else entirely? Or a book you "wrote" in your mind but never put on paper suddenly appears in the bookstores?

Now that you know a little more about Energy and the Law of Attraction, you can see that one of two things is possible:

1. You *could* have originated the idea, fully developed it in your mind (thus making it even more real) and then never took action on it...but the idea had been created. You did not just erase it, so it is just floating around out there. Eventually, someone else may have run into (attracted) that Energy, or was found *by* it when the time was right. They then took **action** on the idea and facilitated it coming into the physical.
2. Or, someone else originated the idea, did nothing with it, and it found it is way to *you*, in search of some means to come in to the physical. You *thought* it was "your idea", but it was out there already. You just *experienced* that it was your idea. Either way, you attracted it! Have you ever just had an idea pop in out of nowhere, with no logical thought process even leading up to it? It was just there. Now you can see how that might happen!

So now that you know this, what do you do with it?

Well, first you have to realize that your inspired ideas are opportunities for you to fulfill your desires. They come to you at the perfect time, and will hang around for the perfect timeframe for you to take action on them to fulfill your desires. If you do not act in that timeframe, the idea will move on to someone else. You will always have this "residual memory" of this idea you had but never acted on, so when you see someone *else* fulfill your idea, you think "Hey, that was MY idea!"

We will never permanently "own" ideas.

So what is the lesson? If you have an idea, act on it, or understand that you are intentionally passing up an opportunity for your ultimate desires to be fulfilled. That is assuming, of course, that you have created a vision to live into; a desire that you actually are working to be fulfilled.

If you *are not* working on a desire, then the ideas you have will simply keep you in the reality which you are currently *unconsciously* creating. That is another reason to be dreaming big, and on purpose, for the things you desire in your life. Because you are creating the perpetuation of whatever you are thinking about the most, whether that is consciously or unconsciously.

Remember that ideas are Energy. Depending on how long and hard you focus on an idea you have, its Energy is going to become all the stronger. The idea is destined for manifestation!

You have the option of being its conduit into the physical. The Universe has determined that this is one of the more efficient ways for you to realize your goal. You can opt to take advantage of the opportunity, or let your Ego give you a thousand and one reasons you can not take action on it. There is not anything good or bad about either option. It is entirely your choice to create whatever you want, when you want!

Now, is every little stray thought a road sign from the Universe? Probably not (although it *is* a "reflection" to some degree of what you're vibrating). I think you understand the types of ideas I am talking about. The ones that seem inspired...or the ones that really get you excited...the ones about which you spend the most time thinking.

These are the ideas with the Power.

And by the way, it does not mean that you have to figure everything out about how to act on that idea. Just claim it, and "be" that it has already happened; that you have already facilitated the manifestation of that idea into the physical, and the *Universe* will then figure out the details on its delivery.

You do not have to figure out where the money is coming from to build any prototypes. You do not have to worry about how Steven Spielberg is going to see your script. **You do not have to worry about anything**. BE that it has already happened, and the Universe will provide.

That is such an important point I am going to say it still again: Do not worry about *how* this will happen. Just turn the whole project over to the Universe, and let it happen. Do not complicate things by trying to intellectualize the whole process from beginning to end, because frankly, the Universe is going to provide a much better plan than we could probably ever figure out ourselves.

I know it is hard to give up that control, even when you want to. Your Ego totally freaks out when you try to do something like that! But just practice doing it. If you find it hard to totally give up control over the manifestation process, then just *pretend* you do not have a problem with it. You will be amazed at how effective that is.

So, if you have an idea...whatever it is, and it really lights you up, do not just stop at thinking about the idea all the time. Add ON to that by thinking that you have already seen this idea through to completion and that it is a wild success. Then do not worry about how things will happen. Just start taking action as ideas occur to you.

Again, the ideas *will* come to you. You do not have to force them, which will in fact keep them from coming or make them difficult to recognize.

And if you start this process then seem suddenly *bombarded* with ideas that begin to propagate into others more quickly than you could possibly take action on, simply choose the one that seems most appealing to you, and take action on that and be totally okay with putting the others on hold, or letting them go completely.

You see, you could say to the Universe, "I desire THIS" - whatever it is - and then suddenly the Universe bombards you with a vast array of possible ways to do this. Just choose one, and you will begin to narrow down your choices. So you choose one, and then the Universe will give you a bunch of ideas on how to act on it.

If you could not possibly do them all, just choose a few that seem appealing and act on those. Do not stress over it, or make it a big deal.

You are going to have your desire fulfilled.

You are simply choosing the path to get there. There aren't any "wrong" choices. ALL choices will get you there...in the most efficient manner possible, based on the choices you make along the way.

Make Friends with Your Ego

Rather than try to destroy it.

By now, you know that your Ego can sometimes work against you in extremely crippling ways. I do not want you to get the idea that the Ego is evil, or your enemy. In fact, it can be a very important ally. It is just that very often, it stands in the way of you fulfilling your destiny. When you are in these situations – where you are intellectualizing everything, or trying to figure things out, or guide the process instead of letting it happen - rather than resisting the Ego, why not just give it all the facts?

Imagine having a conversation with it, to fully explain how things are going to be from now on, and how the Ego will benefit.

Here is one way to do that.

First, fully bring into your experience the feeling of *benefit* you will have when your desire is fulfilled. Make it a fully satisfying experience so you can make the Ego very aware that **this great feeling and even better** can be ours *all the time.* This "feeling", and others like it, is the "payoff" – the bargaining chip, if you will – with your Ego.

If you have got a good image of your dream home – and perhaps you are living there now – find a room that you have significantly developed in the way of detail, and in your imagination, sit across from your Ego and have a conversation something like this.

You: Are you comfortable?

Ego: Yes.

You: Great. I wanted to have a conversation with you because I know things have been pretty different around here lately.

Ego: Yes.

You: I just want to let you know that you are welcome to come along on this journey. I am not trying to leave you behind or sneak around you. I have no desire to trick you, because that wouldn't be permanent, and there would probably be repercussions. I'd just like you to understand how fully satisfying moving forward with these principles is going to be for you. Virtually every desire you have will be fulfilled.

Ego: But I just do not see that happening. Where's the evidence?

You: I have given you tons of evidence. You have READ the evidence. You have experienced the evidence. Recently! You KNOW what I am saying is true.

Ego: No I do not.

You: What are you afraid of?

Ego: (pause) Losing control maybe?

You: What do you mean?

Ego: I mean literally losing control! If every thought becomes manifested – if we REALLY master this stuff – wouldn't it be like living in some kind of virtual reality machine that is out of control?

You: Only if we create our reality to be like that...which would never happen because at a core level, I do not WANT that to happen.

Ego: Ok, I see...because Desire is a key ingredient.

You: Right so just by thinking about something does not mean it is going to suddenly become your reality. You still have to "charge" that thought with some kind of emotion.

Ego: But that does not make sense because you are experiencing situations right now that you do not desire. Why are they happening?

You: Because *you* are keeping us on "auto-pilot". There are some things that you just aren't letting go of that would set us truly free. But we are experiencing certain things right now because that is what you are permitting. In some cases, you are just not allowing things to happen? Why are you doing that?

Ego: I do not know.

You: Well, will you stop?

Ego: I don't know.

You: Look, why don't we just try it my way for a couple of weeks. For two weeks, you just keep quiet and enjoy the experience. You just allow us to create a new and better reality for ourselves. Do not overanalyze things, and do not try to figure things out. Do not evaluate actions. Just allow me to take them without throwing your voice into the mix. I have some incredible ideas that you are going to LOVE experiencing. I promise. You are going to have fun, and feel fully satisfied. Together, we are going to be much more powerful experience-ers and creators.

Ego: Two weeks?

You: Right. Two weeks. With the agreement that when you see how wonderful things quickly become, that two weeks extends forever.

Ego: Ok, I will do that.

So you get the idea. You'll want to tailor your "conversation" to whatever objections your Ego keeps throwing your way. You want to fully comfort the Ego that this is all in his or her best interest, and you make some kind of deal. If the Ego pops in again after making that deal, simply remind it, "Remember the deal. Remember the payoff". And simply continue.

It may be necessary to have follow-up conversations with the Ego, by the way. Just do it! Whatever works to quiet the Ego is very valuable, especially as you first start. This is just one technique you might want to try. Meditation is another. Perhaps you could have this conversation while in a meditative state!

Just do *something* to deal with the objections of the Ego…because they will stop you with reason, logic, and external evidence if you let them. And most of the time we let them because we do not really recognize them for what they are: automatic responses based on false information. Knowing this can take away their power. Soon, they have no power at all, and you are free.

In the Face of all the Evidence

One of the MOST asked questions I get via email is also the toughest one to answer. Not because there is any "trick" to the answer, but because the answer is so often hard to hear and implement for the person who asked. It goes something like this:

"I know we are supposed to think about how we are wealthy, but how can I do that when all around me I have reminders that I am not? I have got more bills than money, and it is really hard to feel wealthy right now."

When people ask me that, I feel like they are hoping I will say something that I have never said before, like there is some secret that I have not yet divulged, or some "shortcut" to the already very simple Law of Attraction principles.

Well, there is not. It does not get any simpler than this: Get into the emotion of feeling wealthy.

So, I can hear you pulling your hair out, right? Ok, let us tackle this "easier said than done" topic.

You have spent your *whole life* integrating beliefs and feelings that have attracted your current situation. You have evidence of "lack" all around you because for years, you have been playing somebody else's game. You have bought into the mass mentality of "there is never enough", and as a result, this has become a belief – a predominant feeling - thus you have **attracted** the circumstances to substantiate this belief. And you have probably done it very well.

So now this book tells you it is simply time to attract something else. So you start chanting affirmations like, "I am wealth. I am abundance. I am joy." But as you are repeating this mantra over and over, you are staring at a stack of bills that you feel you can't pay.

So basically, you are just wasting your time. Because although you are "saying words", your **feelings** and **emotions** are vibrating something totally different. It is just like using any other affirmation that you do not really believe.

And in fact, if your true attention is on your lack, you have probably also got a layer of conversation saying, "All this 'feeling wealthy' stuff is not working. I have been trying, and nothing is working. This is ridiculous. When is it going to happen?"

When you find yourself saying this, it is time to step up and take responsibility. It is not the Law of Attraction not working. You are slowing it down.

You MUST understand that **you** cannot *break* the Law of Attraction. If you are not attracting what you want, it is absolutely because your predominant vibration is attracting something else. Plain and simple.

What do we do about that?

Think about this:

When you were born, you were not born with a lack mentality. It is something that was taught to you over many, many years. Your environment, which supported that belief, was the result of the predominant feelings of *others* who came before you. So if you were not exposed to anything different, how could you have possibly cultivated a belief in infinite and unlimited abundance?

So, as you bought into these belief systems – surrounded by *other people's* evidence as you grew up - you just basically *synchronized* with their vibrations and made them your own. So, you became your very own magnet to lack, and you have been that way ever since.

How long does it take to change this? Ultimately it is up to you. Now, I know that everyone says that the *Universe* decides when and where a desire will manifest, but that will still **always be in direct response to what you are vibrating**. The Universe will deliver appropriately in accordance to what you are magnetizing, and thus allowing.

Here's an example.

Suppose you are $30,000 in debt.

First, you not only have to accept responsibility for the fact that you attracted that debt, but it would also help you greatly to be outrageously grateful for it.

"So tell me again why I am to be grateful for huge debt?"

Because that debt is the exact appropriate response to what you have been vibrating all this time, and it shows you that the Universe does, in fact, respond perfectly! Knowing this, you now have the freedom of choice to vibrate something totally different!

But remember, you have been **feeling** this debt into existence on many levels, probably for many years. Just simply chanting an affirmation about being "wealthy" without any real *feelings* that resonate with those words will result in something that the Universe hears something like this:

"I am Wealthy... I am Wealthy... I easily pay my bills..."

while at the same time hearing:

"30 thousand dollars in debt...30 thousand dollars in debt...30 thousand dollars in debt...How am I ever going to pay it?"

So you have got two conversations running and chances are very good that the *second* conversation about the debt has much stronger emotions connected to it, because it is your experience right now.

So what happens? You attract MORE stress, MORE fear, MORE worry, and possibly even MORE debt because that is what you are truly magnetizing.

You see, it is not that the Law of Attraction is not working for you. It most definitely is working; just not in the way that you consciously want it to.

So what do you do?

Given that most of us cannot completely turn off that negative conversation like a light switch, you have to start small. You have to do what you can to experience the Positive feelings associated with your desire, even if it is just for moments at a time, *because in those moments*, you will be magnetizing more of the same.

The Abraham-Hicks folks, among others, talk about the power of holding a vibration for 17 seconds, then doing it again, and so on, and the exponentially magnetic power of doing that. While 17 seconds does not seem that long, just try to hold your positive feelings for that long without getting distracted with a negative thought. It is not that easy.

However, we DO provide a tool in the next section of this book to help extend the time you can stay in a truly positive and magnetic space, and it is the Experiential Meditation. I get more positive feedback on this meditation than just about any other part of the "Wealth Beyond Reason" program, and I highly recommend that you start making this meditation a daily practice. Simply put, **it makes you extremely magnetic** for the period of time that you are using it. And the more you use it, the easier it will be for you get into the feeling of having what you want, rather than thinking about what you do not want. That feeling will build and build, until eventually the scales are tipped the other way.

However, a couple of things have to be happening at the same time:

One, make sure you are not consciously going back into a state of worry or fear around your money when the meditation is over. That is a *choice* (albeit an easy one) that while habitual, is totally destructive. And if you do that, the bulk of your day will be spent sending out frequencies of worry or fear, and that is what you will get more of.

So my suggestion is this: When you come out of the wonderful feeling of experiencing your desire, no matter how long it lasted, be sure to express your gratitude for your ability to feel that way! And also express your gratitude for everything around you right now, knowing that it is through this wonderful, seemingly magical power of the Law of Attraction, that it is a part of your experience.

Also keep it in the forefront of your mind that you *have* begun to start the trend in another direction, and that although you might have only felt truly prosperous for a few moments, that **you have set magnetic forces in motion** that will bring you are the circumstances in which you can experience more of that feeling, provided you allow it, and do not crowd it out with a lot of intentional negative thinking.

In the meantime though, what do you *do* about the debt, particularly if you do not have the money to pay it?

Well, what CAN you do? If you do not have the money, you do not have the money! Worrying about it will solve absolutely nothing. I know it seems natural and logical to worry about it, but that only because "worrying" is what you have been taught. You have associated all sorts of terrible things with the inability to pay a bill, and as a result you attract those negative things. That is just the way it is.

So pay what you are able to pay, thankful that you can pay that, and with a knowing that extreme abundance is just around the corner.

If you spend the unproductive time you use to worry, on instead creating a vision of prosperity for yourself, rich with the feelings of doing exactly and ONLY what you love doing, your time is much better spent – and you can make no better investment.

Ok, so it is tough at first. So what? Does that mean you should quit? Look, you either *strongly* desire a change in your life, or you are content to keep making excuses as to why the Law of Attraction "does not work for you." Well, *you* are the one making that statement seem true. And the only thing you need to do is to commit to *however long it takes* to turn things around.

It takes practice. And that does not mean just going through the motions, or chanting the "I am wealthy" mantra, because most likely those words by themselves have very little meaning or power for you. Find what you most passionately desire in life, generate the wondrous feelings associated with that, and make those your focus throughout the day. You must, and I mean you *must* watch where you have your attention that is what is attracting your circumstances. Good or bad.

Please, choose to put your attention on happy thoughts. Often. Because the more you do, the easier it will become. It *has* to, because that is how the Law of Attraction works. Every time.

The Experiential Meditation

This meditation works best for the manifestation of actual physical "things" rather than intangible desires like relationships, peace of mind, or happiness.

I recommend that you record yourself reading this meditation so you can conveniently listen to it at any time. I have given instructions on when to pause in your reading. Just a nice, slow, comfortable pace will do the trick! By the way, a fully produced recorded version of this meditation is available as part of the "Wealth Beyond Reason" Internet program.

Before you begin this meditation, you should definitely have a good idea of the desire you want to work on. You should have most of the details worked out on paper. These details should include the full experience of your desire. How you will see it...hear it...feel it...and even taste and smell it if appropriate.

This meditation is designed to *fully* put you into the experience of your desire NOW. The more time you spend with this vision, the quicker you will realize it. You will experience your desire on all sensory levels, including emotion. So before you begin this meditation, you should have at least some vision of these things. That is really important. What you create should be your idea of absolute perfection. It is no harder to create "perfection" than to create something that makes your miserable! So go with perfection and boundless happiness!

Please be sure to give yourself enough time to go through the meditation in its entirety. Make certain that you will not be disturbed and that you are as comfortable as possible. Everything about this experience should be joyous! You do not want to be thinking about anything else, or having any stray worries running in the background. The conditions need to be right to enter into this meditation, because it is extremely powerful.

Getting into a routine would be ideal! Set aside a block of 45 minutes each day, just for creating your reality in this way. It will be an incredibly profitable investment in time, and when you are on a schedule, others will respect that time-slot and you can be assured that you will have the right environment.

This meditation uses a lot of visual imagery. I understand that not everyone currently experiences the ability to visualize clearly. I do believe, however, that cultivating this ability is important. Still, if the images do not come, try this: Simply pretend that you see the images. In other words, imagine what it would be like to see the images. Pretend that you can. The ability to see your imagination visually might just sneak up on you. But in any case, do not worry if you cannot yet create clear pictures. Just immerse yourself in the thoughts and feelings of your desire.

The idea is to immerse yourself in the images, rather that "view" them as if you were watching them on television.

Unlike other meditations, this is not one that you "bring yourself out of" at the end. There are no statements like, "You will find yourself back in your chair..." or anything that would suggest that your current reality is any more real than the one you are creating in the meditation! You will be exactly where you should be in your experience when you are ready to end the meditation. A logical place is when the recording ends, but of course you are welcome to stay in the reality you have created as long as possible!

So if you are ready, get comfortable, get excited about your desire, and let us bring your desire into your physical reality now!

Record the following:

Begin by shifting your awareness to your breathing. Your breaths should be full and natural, and you should have your attention simply on your breath. If your mind should wander just ease your attention back to your breath. We are going to do this for a few minutes to enter a relaxing state. Just keep a natural cycle of cleansing oxygen circulating through your body. Pay particular attention to the space between your breaths...the point where the inhale becomes the exhale...and the exhale becomes the inhale.

Just continue to put your attention on your breathing.

As you lie here, turn your attention to what it feels like physically to exist in your current form. Experience, from head to toe, what it FEELS like to be in the physical at this moment. Try to imagine yourself as a glowing form of Energy. This Energy is taking the form of your body, but only because you are currently creating it that way. Now, however, imagine your body disintegrating into the atomic particles of which it is composed. It feels something like a buzzing, or a vibration throughout your being...almost electric!

The buzz of this Energy gives you a feeling of lightness and freedom. You realize that you are Energy with Infinite possibilities of experience which are determined completely by your thoughts...which interpret this sea of Energy all around you into what you perceive to be your reality.

Now I want you to BE that your desire has been fulfilled. Create the **image** of what that looks like. Focus your full attention on that image in full 3-D as you are there right now. Take the time to fully observe as many details as you possibly can. You are experiencing your desire fulfilled. This is the level of confidence with which you see what you see right now. Your desire has been fulfilled, and you are basking in gratitude and excitement.

You see in bright colors, this new reality you have created simply by shifting your awareness. You are **there**. It is all around you. Of course you see it...it is right in front of you in REALITY...not fantasy.

Spend a moment just really sharpening and enhancing that image.

(PAUSE A BIT)

Choose something in this reality to touch. Touch something and feel the characteristics of its surface. Really experience its texture.

***Feel** its temperature...cool? Warm? Touch as many things as you possibly can that represent the fulfillment of your desire, and really EXPERIENCE the sensation of physical contact.*

(PAUSE A BIT)

***Hear** any sounds associated with the experience of your desire now fulfilled. They are all around you, now! You are now seeing, feeling, and hearing the desire fulfilled.*

*What about **smells**? Think of any smells that you naturally associate with this desire now fulfilled. Fill your being with any aroma you can detect, and as you do, take in a deep breath, and let it out slowly and fully.*

Take another breath, and again bring the reality of your experience into your being...hold it there a moment, allowing your reality to fully permeate you. Then, exhale slowly and fully.

*If there are any **tastes** associated with this desire, add these to your experience. Bring in the flavor of this experience if at all possible. You want to wake up every sensory receptor in your body, and allow it to experience your new reality fully and completely!*

Finally, how do you feel? Amplify the emotions you are feeling now that you have realized this desire. Make the emotions bigger and grander! More excited and joyous!

*And now send out the Energy of extreme gratitude that your desire has been fulfilled so completely and perfectly. Give thanks, and give **more** thanks and FEEL that Energy of gratitude flow out of your being and into the rest of the Universe as a payment for this fulfilled desire.*

*Spend as much time as you want to in this vision. Continue to live the **full sensory experience** of your desire fulfilled. As the music fades away, fully enjoy the knowledge that you have created a new and ultimately fulfilling reality that is yours to step into Now.*

So Now, It is Up to You

Well, I have done everything I told you I was going to do.

I have told you absolutely everything you need to know to create the perfect life. Not just a good life. Not just a *great* life. A Perfect Life.

What will you do now? Will you begin designing your life with intention and commitment, or will you keep waiting for something "out there" to happen? Because until it happens "in here", it will not appear *out there.*

As I have mentioned repeatedly, the Law of Attraction is at work in your life, whether you purposefully "invoke" it or not. Why not **use** this incredible ability, rather than be victim of it?

It is all spelled out in the book you are holding.

But if you still have questions, I am happy to answer them. Refer to the "Contact Us" section of this book to learn how to reach me personally at any time.

Whatever you do, find something to be happy about. Flip on your desire magnet, and start attracting! Make up for all the lost years. Do not live another moment in compromise. Follow your passions. They know the way.

Recommended Resources

Obviously, I do a lot of research on the topic of the "Law of Attraction". A big part of my work on this planet is sharing these ideas in an educational format. That is why this book was written, and why the "Wealth Beyond Reason" online program was created. The "Wealth Beyond Reason" program is available from:

http://www.WealthBeyondReason.com

The basic program consists of a library of *e-books* (books that you download to your computer) on the topic of raising your "wealth consciousness" and utilizing the Law of Attraction as discussed in this book. Obviously, I recommend all the books in the package (or they would not be included). The basic program also includes audio seminars and meditations.

But since putting together "Wealth Beyond Reason", I have found some other extraordinary resources that have helped me personally integrate and experience new levels of success with these principles, and I want to share them with you, all with a high recommendation based on **my personal experience**! I have referred to a few of these works in the content of this book, and the following Internet links will provide even more information on how to obtain this material for yourself! I hope you will take the time to investigate these resources because I truly believe you will find them extremely valuable!

1. **"Wealth Beyond Reason Internet Program"** – *Boundless Living* – This is the "continuing education" program on which this book is based. Members receive ongoing audio seminars and written material, personal coaching, and the opportunity for learning the principles within a structured curriculum which includes "virtual classes" on various aspects of the principles. Includes textbooks, audio seminars, and meditations.

   http://www.wealthbeyondreason.com

2. **"I'm Rich Beyond My Wildest Dreams! I Am, I Am, I Am!"** – *Tom and Penelope Pauley* – A wonderful "handbook" on practically implementing the principles in a regular and practical way.

   http://www.wealthbeyondreason.com/richdreams.html

3. **"The Classic Seed Money In Action"** – *Jon Speller*- Everything you need to know and understand about "giving" and receiving a tenfold return.

   http://www.wealthbeyondreason.com/seedmoney.html

4. **"Merlin's Message"** – *Marelin the Magician* – Small enough to fit in your pocket, this book holds incredible insights and truths related to using the Law of Attraction in your everyday life. A delight to read, and thoroughly life-changing.

   http://www.wealthbeyondreason.com/merlin.html

5. **"The Greatest Money-Making Secret In History"** – *Joe Vitale* – Find out how some of the world's most successful people grew their fortunes through giving.

   http://www.wealthbeyondreason.com/greatestsecret.shtml

6. **"The Have a Nice Day Workbook"** – *Compiled by Ulrike Haupt* – This is a wonderful FREE publication that acts as a handbook for the powerful information available from Abraham-Hicks Publications. This provides a powerful experiential education in the Law of Attraction through daily exercise, and incredible wisdom from Abraham.

   http://www.whatanicewebsite.com/faces

7. **"Abraham-Hicks Publications"** – *Jerry and Esther Hicks* – There is a wealth of information here about the Law of Attraction and how you can apply it to nearly every area of your life! A wonderful search function lets you quickly find wisdom on nearly any topic!

   http://www.abraham-hicks.com

8. **"Wealth Beyond Reason Audio Collection"** – CDs of many of our audio seminars, as well as fully produced versions of our meditations and other seminars, are available for purchase online:

   http://cd.wealthbeyondreason.com

9. **"How to Get Lots of Money for Anything FAST!"** – *Stuart Lichtman and Joe Vitale* This is an incredible course that walks you through practical utilization of the Law of Attraction, without even using the term! If you would enjoy a structured approach to implementing powerful change, this is the perfect course to compliment the "Wealth Beyond Reason" material!

   http://wealthbeyondreason.com/getmoneyfast.php

Contact Us!

We appreciate the opportunity to help guide you through the integration of these principles, and welcome communication from you in a number of ways!

Via the Web:

http://www.WealthBeyondReason.com

Email:

Bob Doyle
bobdoyle@boundlessliving.com

Telephone:

Mobile Office: 800-427-4527
Fax: 720-294-5666

Here is what people are saying about the "Wealth Beyond Reason" Internet program:

"Since I've gotten the "WBR" package I've learned how to identify and "let go" of the negative Energy...this is going to be **an awesome life now**! In one week I have **turned none paying clients into paying clients** and **allowed the manifestation of an $11,000 piece of equipment** that I've been struggling to get since January...all by simply letting go of the negative Energy and feeding the positive Energy. Now I can see a field of wealth particles being magnetically drawn to me constantly...it looks like a star-field...I have actually become a **wealth magnet**!"

Roger Kelly
contactme@rogerkelley.com

"**Utterly Fantastic! Overwhelmingly eye-opening**! I have just completed my first month of the new year and have made this January **THE most productive month financially** in the eight years that I have been in business."

Bobby Allen
bobby.allen@spectrumlending.com

"I must say that I have not been studying the program for very long but so far **the results have been great**!! I was unemployed for the past 3 months and started using the principle of giving for a 10 fold return and it has worked wonders! **I got a job within 2 days of starting the practice** and this was from the $10 purchase of the e-book seed money. **I was also paid $258.00** owed to me from a program I was promoting on the internet that I thought had gone bad. and last but not least yesterday **I won a shopping spree** at a local supermarket!! This stuff is great and I can't thank you enough. God bless you and yours!!"

Michael Tugend
mtugend@adelphia.net

"I cannot tell you how EXCITED I am about this program and your material I have already read. At 50 years old have been through all the books, but it never really sunk in until 2 or 3 days ago when I started reading "**A Happy Pocket Full of Money**" I now think back at the terms or phrases from other material and understand what it all meant. "Think and Grow Rich" is one I read and re-read, but it didn't register. Depak Chopra is another one who confused me, but from the little I have read from your newsletter and the David Cameron book I now understand some of the things he talks about. **Your audio, which I am listening to is AWESOME!** I will definitely use it daily."

Richard Dundon
richard.dundon@verizon.net

-

"The Wealth Beyond Reason program is truly **a gift at any price**. The information has not only awakened me spiritually it has afforded me the opportunity to experience wealth and joy on a daily basis and lifted a huge amount of stress from my life. The information is timeless and **I use it every day**. The truth will set you free and the Wealth Beyond Reason package not only contains the truth, it will expose you to more truth as you work the program!"

Chris Nelson
Cnelso@msn.com

"I've had the course only for a short while and I have noticed a great shift in my consciousness. The Wealth Meditation is **excellent**. The "Happy Pocket Full of Money" is **incredible**. That book has so many gems and insights, I can't seem to put it down. I have a strong feeling at this point that **this program is going to really change my life**. I was very, very skeptical about this program. I had tried many others that claimed all sorts of benefits and delivered nothing. From what I have seen **this course is worth many times its cost**. I would implore anyone who would like to change their financial future to start this course and let the change begin!"

Ray Preisler
drrayman@hotmail.com

"**This is what they should start teaching kids in school**, it would change this country for the better."

Charles Hutchcraft
chutchcraft@hotmail.com

"You have opened the heavens for me. Coming from a religious background I felt like I couldn't "look at God in the eye" anymore. You have restored my faith in the universe, its creator and myself! **I finally feel grounded, excited, and peaceful all in the same time!!** Thank you, and keep it coming!"

Marie-France Dougherty
mfgdougherty@yahoo.com

"The information is truly amazing! (I completed **A Pocket full of Money** and I'm reading it for the second time - want to get everything) I have read a lot of books on spirituality but **your package is the key I have been looking for.**"

James Nwachukwu
ikenna2k@netscape.net

"**I am thrilled** to have purchased the "Wealth Beyond Reason" program last December. I find the Everyday 12-point savers and "A happy pocket full of money" exceptionally helpful in deepen my understanding on **the missing link I've been seeking for the past few years**."

Amy Cheung
http://www.quickenselfhealing.net

"After only a couple weeks reading and absorbing the materials, **I've made some huge shifts in my approach to wealth and finance in my life**. The approach to tithing alone has made a great impact. **Money is showing up now** just to give me the opportunity to start fulfilling my giving goals. It is **amazingly fun and joyful** to give now. I do tell all my friends about this. And, now my friends and I are actually talking about wealth -- a previously taboo subject. **It's wonderful and refreshing.**"

Pat Edwards
pat.edwards@att.net

"Indeed your material (pocket full of money) is the one of the most enlightening books I have ever come across. I have been a Christian now for several years and the information in your book transforms the Bible to here and now. It is so powerful and very effective. Indeed the truth shall set you free. The truth found in your book is parallel with all truths and dispels every myth conceivable to man and breaks every strong hold."

Anthony Da Silva
Tgivj@aol.com

"Just wanted to let you know... this 'Wealth Beyond Reason' is a real gift...consider the value of it far beyond what I paid - easily. The timing couldn't have been more right for it to fall into my hands, too."

Mike Koger
biocybernetics@aol.com

"I have worked on this type of program for over 30 years now. Yours is **the most concise and to the point** that I have run across."

John Bixler, Sr
pabmyname01@comcast.net

"I am very happy to let you know that the "Wealth Beyond Reason" program is **the most enlightening, helpful and motivational program that I have ever had the pleasure to experience**. I say this because, this program is not just another program to purchase and read. It is a true, positive experience."

Deatra Cummings
deacum@attbi.com

"I am really enjoying this material. **It's the best I've ever seen on the subjects**. You really delivered value here."

Doug Abney
prosperking@aol.com

"**Very powerful.** It's perfect for the goal I intend to achieve! Great stuff! I have studied and practiced a number of systems in search of ways to assist clients, in addition to my personal growth, and I must say that **your program is very exciting**. I have just begun to use your seminar, and it is priceless. **My income has already increased**, and for the first time ever, I feel confident that I will achieve my financial goals. Thank-you!"

Sheryl Westergreen
sheryl@visionact.biz

"This is a **wonderful program**. After reading several books on LOA, I thought I couldn't find anything new. This covers a lot of the questions I still had."

Carol Hill
carohill@attbi.com

"I just want to tell you that **my mind has been absolutely blown** and I believe every word of this (Happy Pocket...). It makes everything I've ever believed about God and our true nature make complete sense. **I cannot thank you enough. It is already changing my life.**"

Stacy Simmons
sas@freespeech.com

About the Author

Bob Doyle is the founder of Boundless Living, a worldwide educational personal development company that focuses its work around the Law of Attraction and its role in our lives.

In addition to seemingly non-stop writing, Bob also spends time following his passions of music composition, fitness, and goofing around, enjoying Life.

He highly recommends goofing around as much as possible.

Bob lives in Duluth, Georgia with his wife Krissy, his children, Catharine, Deborah, and Max, and various animals that think they own the place.

Visit some of Bob's other web sites!

BodyChangers - http://www.bodychangers.com

Flightwaves – http://www.flightwaves.com

Boundless Living – http://www.boundlessliving.com

Original Music – http://music.wealthbeyondreason.com

ISBN 141201360-7